Daemonic Prosperity Magick

Ψ

S. Connolly

Daemonic Prosperity Magick

Ψ

S. Connolly

DB PUBLISHING 2018

MMXVIII

DB Publishing is an arm of Darkerwood Publishing Group, PO Box 2011, Arvada, CO 80001.

STANDARD HARDCOVER EDITION

Daemonic Prosperity Magick© 2017-2018 by S. Connolly. No part of this book may be reproduced in any form, electronic or other, without express written permission from the author and publisher. Please respect the author's copyright.

Book Design by Stephanie Reisner

Editorial Acknowledgements: William Briar, L. Hardin, S. Grey

May your rites be well attended, may you be prosperous and blessed, and may the Daemonic dwell within you all of your days. So be it.

CONTENTS

Introduction – 1

Wealth Magick Basics – 8

Opportunity – 22

Seven Important Points – 33

Discipline & Dedication – 35

Passion – 47

Motivation – 52

Magickal Talent – 56

Real-World Talent – 59

Dedication – 67

Money – 79

Five Daemons for Wealth & Success – 100

Sorath – 109

Why Selling Your Soul is Stupid – 118

Why Magick for Money/Success Fails – 121

Common Self Work Required – 123

More Spells & Rituals for Prosperity – 126

INTRODUCTION

Prosperity, wealth and financial magick has been a hot topic in recent years. This book is all about the basics of using Daemonic Magick for the purpose of prosperity. I've had some rather disgruntled readers approach me over the years questioning my methods of sorcery and saying I should put my money where my mouth is. That's the reason for this book. In it I'm going to give you the steps to becoming a financially responsible and stable individual ala Daemonolatry style. I'm not going to lie to you -- you will have to work. You won't get anything by sitting on your ass. If you do - you're lucky indeed.

This book is great for young adults just starting out on their own as well as those who just haven't quite grasped how to manage their finances as adults. A lot of it is common sense. All of it is workable and I am living proof that it works. I have tested each of the rituals and formulas herein multiple times, and have only included those that worked for me one hundred percent of the time.

Of course, I suppose results will depend on each individual magician's work ethic. Those willing to work it will reap the rewards, those not willing to work it will end up just as broke as they were before they bought this book.

So first let me tell you what makes me qualified to write this book.

I have all the things many people aspire to
I make a living doing what I love.
I make a very generous annual salary (but I do work for it).
I own my own home.
I live comfortably (i.e. I am not living paycheck to paycheck).
I have retirement accounts and stock portfolios.
I own three cars and can afford nice vacations.
I have money in savings.

Does this sound like what you'd want for yourself? Good. Keep reading. You can have this too.

I wasn't always in my current income bracket. In my late teens, after I left home, I drove a piece of crap car and lived in a small, cockroach infested apartment on the wrong side of town. But it was all I could afford while going to college. I worked two jobs while in college. I went to school full time and worked part time as an office clerk at two different companies. My income amounted to about $800 a month back then. My rent was $279. The car cost me about $100 a month to operate. Food cost about $100 a month. If I had anything left over, it all went into savings for the following semester of school.

I began working Daemonic magick to improve my situation because I couldn't stand living with roaches. It was disgusting. Mind you I'm not the type to work magick for every little mishap in life either. I only bother the Daemonic with those things that are, in fact, major life overhauls. Probably because I learned early on that magick shouldn't be used as a quick fix to every tiny little problem. I believe in learning how to cope with and navigate problems without magickal crutches when possible. Becoming financially stable, for me, was one of the bigger issues.

Within a month of my first ritual, an opportunity presented itself to where I could move into a tiny, two-bedroom, roach free house for $400 a month. I knew that if I could find a roommate, it would only cost me $200. I jumped at the opportunity. After all, it was $79 less a month and roach-free! Over coffee one morning I mentioned to a female friend who worked in the same building that I did, that I needed a roommate. It turned out that she needed a new place to live. Voila! A month later, I had a new place and I was saving money. I also went to both of my bosses and asked for raises, and got them. My income increased to about $900 a month. I was $179 ahead of the game instantly.

But here's also what I didn't do:
I didn't spend money on entertainment or hobbies.
I didn't drink my money away.
If I wanted to buy something big or expensive, I went without until I saved enough for it.
I didn't have credit cards.

Each time I'd work Daemonic magick for financial gain or prosperity, I'd be presented with a new opportunity and each time I'd take the opportunity and run with it, while simultaneously being smart about my financial choices. Each time - I found I was able to upgrade my life a little bit more.

Ultimately by the time I graduated college I was living in a nice one-bedroom condo, I had no student loan debt, I had a nicer car, and I had a little extra money to spend on luxury items like new clothes, going out to dinner with friends, etc...

It happened in small baby steps. See, I think part of the problem our modern culture presents is that Americans (if you're an American) want instant gratification. We want what we want when we want it, and when we want it is usually right now. We are not a culture known for our patience. Getting to a place of prosperity may not happen overnight.

One of the things I want to get out of the way before we discuss the rituals in this book is that the rituals themselves may not seem very elaborate. Some of them may even appear basic. But then the point of these rituals is not for them to look pretty or read like poetry. The point is for them to be useful, and to actually work. Over the years, I've found that excessive lamentation or oration does not work as well as deep meditation, ascension practice, and intent driven spell work. Pulling together magickal timing, herbs, stones, Daemonic forces, and intent is usually enough to make the workings herein manifest. Some people may enjoy more elaborate ritual, in which case the rituals may be modified to your personal preference. You are free to experiment. Nothing in here is written in stone and rituals don't necessarily need to be precise in order to work. Use your foundational knowledge of magick, tools, and different techniques to modify. Remember, books are simply collections of ideas meant to inspire your own Great Work.

I am assuming the magicians using this book at least have a foundational practice of meditation that already exists in their life. If you do not, I highly suggest you begin meditation as a daily practice. Meditation is a foundational skill for all magick. If you do not have this foundational skill, you will find the meditations in this book inaccessible because I don't handhold the magician and teach him how to meditate. Meditation is also necessary for energy work.

Now on to some commentary about the rituals. For all rituals in this book you will need a quiet place to work where you will not be interrupted. This is important because it gives you time to focus on your priorities and desires.

Do not worry if you do not feel as though a Daemonic presence has shown up for the work. Some people do not feel Daemons as acutely as others. Sometimes Daemonic energy blends so well with your own that you may a mistake it for not being there at all. You may think your ritual was not well attended when the opposite is actually true. Most of the magick in this book will manifest within a week. If you find a ritual has not manifested in that time frame, feel free to repeat it. All the while, remember to follow through with any magick you do for the best results.

Results will vary depending on individual work ethic and dedication to the practice.

This leads me to discuss what you should be expecting.

Your Expectations

This is the most important part of this book and you'll find some of this repeated throughout the book because it's important. If you read nothing else, read this. Many of you already know this, but for those who don't: **Daemons are not a quick fix to all your financial or career problems**. Sorry, but they're not. If that's what you're looking for, throw this book into the trash bin.

Defining realistic expectations can be hard. Especially when we're pelted with fictional tales of Daemonic theophany and soul selling to get what we want. Let's talk a little bit about how Daemons work and what kind of expectations are realistic.

How Do Daemons Work?

Divine Intelligence works to help us make better choices, find opportunities, gather strength to accept opportunities, and to face our fears and become better, stronger, and more able to manifest our will. This means that Daemonic influence, whether it manifests in a good way, or a bad way, is often in our best interest. For some people, when the magick manifests with bad or hurtful results, this makes the Daemons appear to be evil, and/or liars. I assure you, however, they are neither of those things. Daemons are lesson teachers. Magick won't always manifest in the way we want, but I guarantee you that you're going to learn something from it and end up a better or stronger person because of it. Sometimes certain areas of our lives need to go up in flames (figuratively) and be destroyed in order to lay new foundational work for something better. Something that serves us.

Remember that life is not something that happens to you — YOU happen to your life. You are the master of your own path and very little happens in your life without your approval. So, when bad things happen, ask yourself what you can learn from it. Then learn from it. Do your best to not continue making the same mistake, otherwise the Daemons will keep throwing opportunities for you to make that same mistake over and over again until you learn. They're lesson teachers. In order to grow and change we need to have our comfort zones challenged. When you're in your comfort zone, nothing changes. We can either challenge ourselves or we can resist challenges, and the Daemons will force challenges upon us. The question is, do you want your challenges on your own terms, or theirs? That is your choice.

How to Define Your Expectations

You get out of anything what you put into it. This applies to most things in life from education to careers. Desire + Dedication + Persistence + Effort = Results. Your individual work ethic is a good place to start when you begin to wonder what your realistic results should look like. Do you just want manna from heaven (or hell I suppose) to appear on your doorstep, ripe for the plucking? Sure, you can see windfall results with Daemonic magick of the Daemonolatry variety. But the results will often be short lived.

Before we start, you need to be completely honest with yourself.

How do *you* define the words prosperity, wealth, and abundance? What images and feelings do these words evoke? What is your real reason for seeking prosperity?

Whatever prosperity looks like to you — that is going to change what your expected results look like.

If you set your expectations too high, you set yourself up for extreme disappointment. If you set them too low, you may not feel as compelled to apply effort to the cause. The trick is defining exactly where you want to be and setting realistic, attainable goals. We will talk more about that later.

So, let's get to it, shall we?

Chapter 1
Wealth Magick Basics

Time and time again I meet magicians (and non-magicians) whose main goal in magickal practice is to bring success, wealth, and prosperity into their lives. They think they can sell their soul for fame or do a quick spell, and if all goes right, money and success will just fall from the sky into their laps with little effort on their part. Some even go as far as to hire other magicians to bring them fame and fortune because they're too damn lazy to do the work themselves. Unfortunately - rarely does it work that way. Sure, we all hear tales of that one magician who threw himself to the flames of Sorath, or who sold his soul, and suddenly had fame and fortune within months. If that ever does happen, it's a rare occurrence. Though I contend it's likely something that doesn't happen at all. It's an urban legend, a myth, much like Doctor Faustus conjuring Mephistopheles and trading his soul for fame. It's fiction, and here's why:

The want for wealth also means the want of work for wealth and this is why so many people who do magick for wealth don't get it. Sure - petitioning Belphegor or a similar Daemon will certainly produce quick cash in short spurts, but long-term sustainability requires you give the Daemonic something to work with. Just like doing a spell to lose weight isn't going to cause you to drop fifty pounds overnight, a few million isn't likely to show up on your doorstep the morning after you do a wealth spell or ritual. You have to be actively pursuing that particular goal and focusing your will on what's important to you in order to achieve success.

This basically means that if you're a shiftless layabout with no ambition or prospects - you will never reach your full prosperity/wealth potential because you're not invested enough in yourself and your own success. It's great to say, "I want to be successful and wealthy." Then the question is -- for what? What do you want to be successful in? By what means will you become wealthy? Because let's face it - not everyone can suddenly find themselves on a reality show making tons of cash just for being pretty. There aren't enough of those positions open. So, you better have a talent, a skill, an idea, or a passion by which to gain wealth.

I always warn that leaving your wealth up to the Daemonic can often result in unexpected situations. I will discuss this more later. The Daemonic is good at making us face our fears so they can teach us lessons. The lesson that most successful and wealthy people learn is that wealth can be fleeting, and it takes hard work and dedication to maintain success. If you aren't willing to do that, wealth, of the monetary sort, may never be yours and you will never be able to grace the world with your full potential.

Now I have a few questions for you to ponder as you read this book:

1. Don't you, and doesn't the world, deserve your passion?
2. What does wealth really mean to you?
3. What does success really mean to you?
4. What does prosperity mean to you?

These answers are going to be different for everyone. Sometimes prosperity means having enough, and for those who would truly be happy with *enough,* a comfortable income and a comfortable career, that's often all they'll ever be able to manifest for themselves. That's not such a bad thing. Being comfortable is highly under-rated in my humble opinion. Because the truth is, for the bulk of us, we just want a roof over our heads, food in our stomachs, a decent job and income, and time to spend with our loved ones. Make sure you really understand the degree of prosperity you're actually seeking. Hence the reason for those questions. After all, money, wealth, prosperity and success in and of themselves rarely make a person happy. Most people have to feel useful and content in what they do in order to be truly happy and to feel successful.

I use myself and my own life as examples a lot in my writing because I'm trying to illustrate points, so please know that when I do this, I'm not bragging. I'm simply trying to serve as an example. When it comes to prosperity, I'm definitely not a bad example.

While I, admittedly, am not a millionaire, I do not aspire to be. When I look at money, I view it as a means to a comfortable life. Not a goal in and of itself. I am comfortable financially, and I'm comfortable financially because I love what I do for a living and I'm good at it. It's hard to make a living in any creative field and writing is no exception. But I've learned over the years it can be done if you're willing to write ad copy and the occasional corporate company policy. When you look at your desired career, a place where your talents can prosper, don't overlook less dramatic contributions because those could be mini-success drawing opportunities. If you're a musician, creating pieces you can license out for commercials or films may seem like selling out, but it could be a lucrative side income to bring attention to your real passion - your music. For artists, using one's skills in advertising could be just as lucrative for you as that big New York art show. You get the gist.

If you are someone looking to a career that doesn't traditionally make money, consider that you might also need to have a regular day job on the side until you hit the right opportunity that will catapult you into your desired career full-time. Many an actor has spent his days working as a waiter or waitress. I still keep a part-time day job in the same field I've worked in for over twenty-five years because I like health insurance. Even though I do make a decent living as a novelist, as I am in a high salary range for a writer, it isn't enough to solely support a family in today's economy. This is where the part-time day job kicks in that extra to keep the family happy, healthy, and able to have the little extras like needed health insurance and the not-so-needed pizza night.

So how do you get to the top of your non-traditional career? Passion and persistence. Of course, neither of these things is exclusive to creative professions. Those who start their own businesses are usually passionate about what they want to do, whether it's brewing beer, having their own law firm, or opening a bakery. When you love what you do, regardless what that thing is, you can take that passion to your business and build success.

Finding your skills, and being honest about those skills is another key component to finding your success. Maybe you are a fantastic nurse, or you make a damn good roast duck. Maybe you could sell anyone swampland in Florida. Once you find that skill and accept your passion for it, you can go on to hone that skill and make a career from it.

One thing I want to point out here, because it's important, is that failure and rejection are all part of success. Most people who are successful can tell you stories about how many times they failed before they made it. So never look on failure as the end of your career. If you do that, and give up because of it, you've cheated yourself.

Yeah, you heard me — YOU CHEAT YOURSELF every time you allow a failure to hold you back. If you love something, and I mean truly love it, then you will persevere and go on despite your failures until you succeed.

So, what is your passion? Is it a part of you? Do you write music or song lyrics? Do you craft beautiful widgets? Is your passion coding video games? Or maybe you like fashion or sales. Everyone is good at something - you just have to find what that something is - then find the right way to capitalize on it. That requires experimentation, taking opportunities when presented, and finding a new path to the same desired outcome if one (or many) ideas fail.

You may be wondering when we get to the Daemonic magick. Hold on. There are still a lot of things you need to think about before you don your robes, brandish a wand, and go jumping into the magick circle.

Before you utter a single invocation, the first step on your path to success and prosperity is to plan it all out on paper.

The ancient Egyptians thought all writing was a magickal act to some degree because the second you start committing your thoughts to paper, that is the first step toward the manifestation of an idea. Let's face it, if you aren't already successful and prosperous, then you only have the idea of being successful and prosperous. Ideas are great, but you have to actually act upon them.

This, of course, is where goal setting comes in. I have discussed goal setting briefly in *The Daemonolater's Guide: Sex, Money, and Power*. We're going to go a little deeper in this book because I think planning and goal setting are extremely important when it comes to prosperity. We need a clear goal of where we're going and how to get there. After all, if someone gives you an address in another state and you're tasked with getting there, you'd use a GPS or a map, right? Why should reaching success be any different? You need a map. For those of you who never use a map and never ask for directions, stop it right there. I am the nagging voice inside your head telling you to stop and ask for directions. Whether it's Daemonic Direction or direction from a human mentor, if you don't know the way to get where you're going, you're going about it the long way around. Why not just swallow your pride and get a little help and input to cut your trip mileage?

I'm not saying you can take a short cut, but sometimes it's easier to take advantage of someone else's experience by asking questions and learning from the answers, than trying to feel your way through blindly. In the case of human mentors, they've already made some mistakes. That doesn't mean that they will keep you from making your own mistakes (because you will make them), but it may cut down time consuming mistakes that discourage you or throw you off track for years at a time.

By having a plan, a goal, and steps to reach each goal, you can figure out the information and advice you need for a successful journey.

Let's start with an example. Let's say you love baking, and armed with great Granny Mavis' recipe book, you want to open your own bakery. What a glorious dream this is. You would be your own boss, make your own hours, and be able to do what you love. In your fantasies, all the hard work and potential pitfalls melt away leaving you with thoughts of wistfully spending your days elbow deep in flour and steeped in the scent of warm breads and cookies. The thing is, realistically you know it's a huge thing and you're going to struggle, and there's business licenses, and building rent, and loans, and whether or not you'll have enough customers to actually buy your baked goods once you get there. And this is likely why you haven't thrown caution to the wind and sunk your entire life savings into a bakery just yet. It seems tempting to just wave your magick wand and poof - instant successful bakery, but even that is beyond Daemonic wish-granting. It's not beyond Daemonic influence though.

So, let's set some goals for our example bakery aspirant. Goals come in three main flavors. Immediate goals, short-term goals, and long-term goals. Immediate and short-term goals are always the most realistic because they're the building blocks to reach long-term goals. Long-term goals can be grand, lofty, and even unrealistic, but you'll find that once you start completing your immediate and short-term goals, the long-term goals may seem more within reach because you're going to revise them on a regular basis. That means you'll kick out goals that are no longer relevant and insert goals that are.

Start with a clean sheet of paper and break it into three sections. Label the first section LONG-TERM. Label the second SHORT-TERM. Label the third IMMEDIATE.

You always begin with the long-term goals, because it's the long-term goals that will dictate what your short-term and immediate goals are. For reference, let's look at long-term goals as goals that are 5+ years into the future. Short-term goals are 1-5 years in the future, and immediate goals are within a year. So, our aspiring bakery owner might have on his/her long-term goal list:

LONG-TERM:
Be supplying local restaurants with cakes and cookies.
Be generating a profit in my local community.
Catering events with baked goods and cakes.

Then we'd move on to steps needed to take to get to these long-term goals.

SHORT-TERM:
Get loan for a bakery.
Get business license for the bakery
Establish a bakery. (Buy or rent a building? Make sure it's zoned properly.)
Advertising for the bakery.
Hire employees?

Feel free to throw notes in there with question marks or concerns you might have with each goal.

IMMEDIATE:
Develop a business plan.
Find a property.
Find out how much all equipment and supplies will cost.
Find out what I have for collateral on a loan. What do I own!?

You could go back through these lists and prioritize each item with numbers, one being the most important and so on. Clearly you need the business plan that includes location and the cost of all equipment and supplies before you go to a bank and ask for a loan.

From the goal list, you can now create actionable to-do lists to accomplish each of these goals. One thing that all successful people have in common is they keep a schedule and they write things down. Start practicing right now by buying yourself a day planner and filling it with your goals and to-do lists. Spend a few minutes each day going over your planner and adjusting things as you go. Spend an hour every Sunday night planning your coming week. You may just find you become more productive and more thoughtful about those things you truly want. You may also discover that there are some things you don't want as badly as you thought you did.

Okay, I know. You've read almost twenty-five-hundred words already and not a damn one of them has included summoning Belial to bring you a pot of gold. Not a single piece of dark poetry or weird incantations. Let me rectify that right now. The following are a meditation and a talisman you can use to draw Daemonic influence and insight into your goal setting process. After all - getting Daemonic insight can help you along the way.

Belial's Sound Business Advice
(for insight into your goals or plans)

This meditation will help you get solid business advice from Lord Belial. Of course, it requires a basic knowledge of how to at least get into the astral temple. It is in your astral temple that you will find Belial for counsel. If you do not have an astral temple you need to come back to this ritual at a later time. It would be both repetitive and exhausting for me to go through the process of creating an astral temple here. I have discussed the astral temple and how to build it in the books *Drawing Down Belial* and *Lake of Fire: A Demonolater's Guide to Ascension.*

It is always a good idea to go into this meditation knowing exactly the answers you're looking for. In this case, perhaps have your business plan ready, or have a specific idea in mind, whether it be a product or marketing strategy.

If you are new to the practice of Demonolatry I do recommend constructing an elemental circle. The reason we often support this notion is so that beginners to the practice do not find themselves unbalanced by the Daemonic energy that they're working with. However, if you have worked with Belial before and you know how you react to his energy, it is okay to skip it. For those of you seeking more active energy during this meditation/Ascension, feel free to construct your ritual space in a way that is pleasing for you.

In a quiet room, dim the lights, and placed the seal of Belial (Dukanté or Goetic, it doesn't matter) in front of you. Flank this by two candles. If you associate green with money or even creativity, these candles can be green. You may also use black or white. They can be tealights or votives or tapers. It doesn't matter. Make sure you're comfortable in the room is at ambient temperature. During the practice of Ascension/meditation is often common to find that your extremities get cold. Being that Belial is the fiery part of earth, some of you may feel heat instead of cold. But this will vary from magician to magician.

Take three, deep measured breaths and relax your body. Imagine all of the tension flowing out of you into the earth. You may choose to think or say aloud Belial's Enn.

"Lirach Tasa Vefa Wehlc Belial"

Imagine the world slowly fading out of focus around you until you find yourself sitting in a dark space. The vast black void around you is all-encompassing and you may begin to feel yourself as nothing more than a tiny pin point of light, insignificant to the rest of the universe that extends far beyond the temple of the mind. Before you, imagine the seal of Belial glowing as an intense bright light. Behind this sigil apparears a doorway that leads to the astral plane, upon which sits your astral temple.

Once you can clearly see the door behind the sigil, feel yourself rise away from your body until you feel weightless and can no longer feel the physical body. The time that it takes to do this will vary from practitioner to practitioner. Now, step through the door into the corridors or hallways that lead to the astral realm. When you find yourself on the astral plane, go to your temple and enter. Some people don't need this much visualization to get to the astral temple, but in this case, take your time getting there - all the while carrying with you your ideas and thoughts about your business as well as meeting Belial there. The longer you focus on this the easier it will be to have your questions answered by the Daemon.

When you enter your astral temple, look around and chances are you will find Belial already there. If not, imagine his sigil hanging over the altar, and invoke him using his Enn. Once he appears to you, explain your situation and ask for his advice. He will openly and freely give his opinion of your ideas and perhaps even make suggestions. Allow this conversation to go on for as long as it needs to. Once you have finished you may pull yourself out of the astral and hence out of Ascension.

Some people draw themselves out of Ascension by simply tapping their own knee, or pulling themselves back from the astral into their bodies with a word, sound, or feeling. Use whichever technique works best for you. You can also use the same technique to speak with any Daemonic force you wish to speak with, for whatever reason.

Belphegor Money Magnet
(to help secure loans and financial backing)

The Belphegor Money magnet is actually a talisman. First, draw the seal of Belphegor on a piece of paper so that you have it handy. Next, gather up a circular piece of wood, or a piece of green/yellow clay and form it into a circular shape. Next, draw, burn, or carve the seal of Belphegor onto it while chanting his Enn, internalizing your want to draw money to you, and then placing that desire into the talisman by pushing through you, through your intent and desire, into your hands, and into the talisman. Spend at least fifteen minutes charging the talisman with your intent. Go longer if you can. If you're using clay you can now bake the clay so that it hardens. If you plan on wearing this talisman make the necessary adjustments (i.e. hole for jump ring etc...). When the talisman is made and ready, bring it back into the temple.

You will need:

- One Lancet device
- Your loan papers (if desired)
- The Talisman
- A sheet of paper
- A pen
- One candle (any color, but green, brown, or black are preferred.)
- An offering bowl suitable for burning a request.

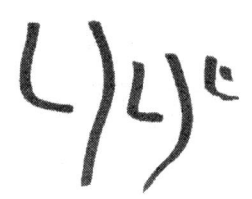

For those new to the practice of Demonolatry, construct an elemental circle and invoke Belphegor from the center. If you are not using an elemental circle, or a ritual construct of your design, simply say the invocation (Enn) of Belphegor.

On the sheet of paper write down exactly what you're seeking. If it's financial backing, investors, a bank loan, or private loan, be specific about what you want. Write it down and sign your name to it. Then, to the right of your name draw the seal of Belphegor. Now leave the paper on the altar or work surface for the moment.

Next, raise the talisman out in front of you. Then say over the talisman:

"Belphegor bring to me the funds I need to [insert specific detail of that here]. Make my venture prosperous and draw favor upon me. For this I offer up my blood."

Now prick your finger with a lancet, and place a drop or two of your own blood on the back of the talisman. For those opposed to blood magick, my recommendation is to not work with Belphegor at all. Belphegor does require the sacrifice of a few drops of your own blood when you work with him. He may still answer your requests without it, but you're going to get the best results with your own blood. Women may use menstrual blood, and you can always pick a scab to get blood if you don't want to prick yourself.

Now squeeze out a drop of blood onto the sheet of paper on top of your signature, and over his sigil. If you need to prick yourself again, do it.

Once the blood has dried, invoke Belphegor over the talisman one more time. Set it on top of the request for five minutes while visualizing your intent. Next, set the talisman aside and burn the request in the offering bowl.

Once this is complete you can close the ritual by thanking Belphegor and any other Daemons present and extinguishing the candle. The talisman itself can be carried with you, worn, or left on your altar.

If you chose to bring your loan paperwork into the temple with you (to draw that Belphegor energy to it before you turn it in to your banker), you may set that upon the altar and place the talisman over a period of at least twelve hours.

Talismans like this can also be made to draw money to you. See the spells and rituals for prosperity section to see more about money drawing.

Chapter 2
Opportunity

Most successful people, if they're smart, are opportunists. The word *no* is used very sparingly in their vocabulary. The question is -when opportunity knocks do you give in to fear and say *no*? Or do you say *maybe...* or even *yes* no matter how much saying *yes* scares the shit out of you?

I have a friend who has always been an aspiring author. She's also loved dogs for as long as she can remember. She has spent her life working with her canine companions and when she was in her early twenties, she started teaching dog training classes at a local shelter. From all of her time spent with her dogs, she began to understand their behavior, and had the privilege of working with some of the country's top animal behaviorists. Because she was a personal friend of some of them, she was able to attend their seminars for free, and by the time she was in her late thirties, she had absorbed a lot of this knowledge and had become a leading canine behaviorist herself. She began traveling the country giving her own seminars on dog training and behavior to help owners better understand man's best friend. It was also an opportunity for her to begin writing a book about canine behavior. Because she already had the huge following in dog-training circles, her first book sold like hotcakes, further throwing her into the spotlight.

Of course, while she loved dogs, she also really loved writing and what she really wanted to write were romance novels. Then, one night after reading a shifter romance (i.e. werewolves) and finding herself pissed at the irregular canine behavior of the wolves in the stories - she had an idea. Knowing canine behavior as she did, she could write a shifter romance that was actually correct when it came to canine behavior. She wrote her first shifter romance and it took off. Notice how two seemingly unrelated interests catapulted her into her desired career and ultimately her success. It was because she took what she loved and threw everything she had into what she loved that the opportunities came and lifted her up. She was wise enough to see those opportunities for what they were, and she took them!

Truthfully, success can happen without magick. I'm sure my dog loving, romance writing friend wasn't sitting in her basement burning candles and invoking Cerberus to make this happen, but had she - I am willing to bet she would have found her career a little faster or found a more immediate path to success.

Aside from giving us direction and helping us find financial backing for our success, Daemons can help highlight or bring forth opportunities that can catapult us to our success faster.

But sometimes opportunities aren't seen for what they are, and so we ignore them or don't follow up on them. We don't see the big picture until someone points it out to us. I have another friend who, due to her expertise on the paranormal, had been contacted for years by television shows seeking to have her on for interviews, or to go ghost hunting with established paranormal groups. But because she's older and overweight, and she's somewhat an introvert, she had the habit of flat out refusing offers to appear on television. She considered it "selling out" and refused to cheapen her experience and knowledge by going on a show where all the paranormal activity was likely staged anyway. She is also an established author on the subject. Sharing the latest producer's offer with a friend, her friend offhandedly suggested that appearing on television might help sell more books and bring her to the attention of even bigger publishers, which was my friend's ultimate goal. (Sorry for all the writer stories, but I know a lot of writers.)

My friend took this advice to heart because, more than anything, she wanted to see her work published by one of the big five [publishers]. So, she swallowed her pride and decided to play the game. After appearing on a paranormal show, she was able to use that to secure a contract offer for one of her fantasy series from a big five publisher, and hasn't looked back since. But it took one of her friends pointing out the benefit of the opportunity to her, to help her realize what an opportunity it was.

How many opportunities have you passed up just in the last year alone? Did you pass it up because you didn't feel qualified? Because you were afraid? Because you didn't think you could do it? I spent one year, on the advice of Leviathan (my Patron), saying yes to every opportunity I was presented with. 2005 was, by far, the scariest year of my life because it involved so much public speaking, which I used to be terrified of. But ultimately it led to bigger and better things and I have never regretted it. I've looked back on it with some embarrassment, yes, but never regret. And now, over eleven years later, I can say with certainty that I am a much better public speaker.

Sure, some opportunities may not lead to anything big, but they are opportunities for experiences. Look at opportunities, especially the scary ones, as a way to learn and prepare yourself for bigger things to come.

You might be asking yourself right now if there is a way to divine which opportunities will give you the most reward for your time and effort. I'm glad you asked because picking and choosing which opportunities to take and which ones to decline is a good occasion to practice your divination skills. You might also want to work with summoning Daemons to bring worthwhile opportunities to you.

At this point I always get the question: "Why not skip all this crap and just use divination to win the lottery, place winning bets, or play the stock market? Screw goal setting and opportunities and all that."

The most primary reason for this is that not all magicians have the ability for such precise divination, and oftentimes, divination doesn't work like that. The gift is not always that "direct." However, I have known plenty of people who have used magick to win bets, the lottery, and do well in the stock market. Because not everyone has that "talent", not everyone can do that kind of magick. An important thing to remember is that none of this usually creates lasting wealth anyway. But opportunities are handy - and they're one of the best ways to draw foundational success that can last a lifetime.

Ba'al's Opportunity Draw

The opportunity draw is an interesting ritual because it's probably not for everyone. I was given this ritual by a friend who heads a coven whose Patron is Ba'al. The premise is much like a spirit vessel where you put elements pleasing to the Daemon in the vessel to draw the energy of that specific Demonic force to you. Usually spirit vessels are left on the altar to influence magick. These bottles work much the same way except on a larger scale. This ritual is actually formulated for people who own their own property. I suppose those who are apartment dwellers, or who live in duplexes, can modify this ritual to use earthen containers in all four corners of their home in which they will bury these "magnet" bottles. As with all Ba'al deities, blood is a component in this ritual. Again, you can draw the blood using a lancet device.

I found this ritual works great for people who are creative and looking to draw inspiration, readers, buyers, or money into their lives.

You need:
- 4 small glass bottles that can either be capped or corked. Wash and dry them thoroughly first.
- 4 small hand drawn sigils of Ba'al on parchment. They need to fit the size of the bottle. Have them created and cut out before you start.
- One cinnamon stick, finely grated.
- A sprig of dried mint (that will easily crumble between your fingers) or a teaspoon of dried mint.
- A teaspoon of solar sea salt.
- Double-sided tape.
- 1 small black candle, one of those charm candles should do the trick.
- A Lancet.
- A piece of parchment or paper.
- A pen.

- Offering Bowl, make sure it's clean.
- A small trowel.
- 4 pots filled with potting soil (optional – for if you're in an apartment, and yes you could probably use houseplants, the bottles should not affect their growth).

For those new to practicing Daemonolatry, construct an elemental circle. More advanced practitioners can construct the ritual space as they wish or just do this ritual as it is written. From each elemental quadrant invoke Ba'al using his invocation (Enn):

Ayer Secore On Ca Ba'al

Light the candle. Take a few moments to center yourself and concentrate on the type of opportunities you would like to draw to you. This is a long-standing ritual, so choose which type of opportunities you're seeking carefully. This is not the type of ritual you would do to attract one-time opportunities. So, if you're looking to attract more business, more money or more creative inspiration, concentrate on that.

On the piece of blank paper write down exactly the type of opportunities you would like to draw. Sign your name at the bottom and to the right of that place the Seal of Ba'al.

Set this aside then uncap each of the bottles. Before using the bottles be sure you have washed and dried them completely. Pick up each bottle, one of the time, whisper the invocation of Ba'al into each of them, and firmly visualize your intent, pushing this energy through you into the bottle through your hands. Then, into each bottle place a pinch of the sea salt, a pinch of the cinnamon, and a pinch of the mint.

Using the Lancet device, prick your finger and place a drop of blood in each bottle. You may need to prick yourself more than once. Finally, add one drop of blood to the written request. I like to smear blood over my signature and over the sigil. While still focused on your intent to draw the opportunities, burn the request in the offering bowl until it is reduced to ash. Once the ashes are cooled, evenly distribute the ashes of the request amongst the four bottles.

Cap each of the bottles. Again, take up each of the bottles, one at a time, into your hands and whisper the invocation of Ba'al at the bottle while visualizing opportunities coming to you. Now take the candle and pour wax over the cap, sealing the bottles.

Take up the seals you made and afix one on each of the bottles using the double-sided tape. At this point you will have four bottles of opportunity draw. If you are working within a circle, thank the Daemons present and extinguish the candle. Don't say goodbye to Ba'al yet!

Next, go outside to the northmost quadrant of your property and hold the first bottle on high. Invoke Ba'al with his Enn. Then, using your hands or a small trowel, dig a hole and place the bottle inside, and then bury it. With your finger trace the Seal of Ba'al in the dirt over the now buried bottle. Repeat this for the other three quadrants working from North to East to South, and finally to West.

Then stand somewhere near the middle of the space where the bottles are placed and imagine the energy of Ba'al bringing those opportunities to you. You can supplement this by asking Ba'al to also give you the wisdom to recognize the opportunities as they are presented so that none are missed.

Once this is done thank Ba'al.

Remember that during every part of this process you should be focused and concentrating on the opportunities you wish to draw to yourself. If you're running a business, you can bury these bottles around the building. Most people just do it around their homes. For apartment dwellers do the same thing just in the small pots of soil (or potted plants) around your apartment. You should begin seeing manifestation of opportunities rather quickly.

This ritual can be applied to other uses and other Daemons as well. If you want to make sure you can find the bottles to dig them up later and disassemble them, be sure to mark them. You might even use planters on your property, but ideally, if you are able, they should be buried in the earth for that connection.

There is an alternate Ba'al Opportunity Draw in the Spells and Ritual Section.

Ashtaroth's Divination to Ascertain a Good Opportunity

First, it is very important that you understand what type of ability you possess with regard to divination, and you know which divination devices work best for your type of ability. The type of divination device you will use in the following ritual will depend on this. If you are unsure, your best bet is likely a pendulum. (See *Drawing Down Belial* for more information.)

It is imperative that the magician knows how to use his or her divination device competently. The reason for this ritual is that before you make a decision on any opportunity, you want to make sure it's a good one. In my experience, the one thing that happens when we use Daemonic forces to draw opportunity to us is that we will be hit with a great deal of opportunity in one shot. Sometimes you can't say yes to every single thing that comes along. It would be virtually impossible. (If you saw what happened with my Sorath model, you would totally understand where I'm coming from here. It can be extremely overwhelming.) That's where this little ritual comes in. When you have too many opportunities and can't take them all on – you need a way to pick and choose.

Now by telling you that you can use this ritual, it doesn't mean you have to. After all, you have a brain and you can use logical, deductive reasoning skills to pick and choose your opportunities based on what you think will benefit you most. However, sometimes two equally good opportunities come up and for whatever reason you know that you can only devote yourself to one of them.

For example, I had opportunities to attend two different events over the same weekend. Obviously, I cannot be in two places at once. They were both about the same distance from me, and both had comparable audience sizes. The difference was one of these events leaned more toward the cozy mystery side of things, while the other leaned more toward the urban fantasy crowd. I market some of my fiction to both audiences, so I was honestly at a loss which event to attend. This ritual helped me out. Astaroth gave me some deeper insight into the situation that suggested my work would be better received by the urban fantasy readers, a younger – hipper crowd of folks. So that's the event I chose, and I ended up selling half a case of books and getting several dozen newsletter subscribers from the deal, many of who went on to buy some of my books on Amazon. Not a bad deal, right? Of course, I wondered what would have happened had I attended the convention full of cozy mystery readers, many of them more mature and with more practical sensibilities. Later discussions with friends who write similar books to mine, and who attended the other event, reported that paranormal cozies didn't do very well at that convention.

So Astaroth was right. I am confident now that the divination session pointed me in the right direction.

Now, onto the ritual. It's actually rather simple. First you need the sigil of Astaroth, and second the Enn of Astaroth

Enn: *Tasa Alora foren Ashtaroth*

You Need:

- 4 white candles
- 1 divination device (pendulum works fine for this, but if you use a pendulum, bring a paper and pen)

Arrange the candles in a semi-circle in front of you. Invoke Astaroth using the Enn. Place her sigil at the base of the candles.

Now take your divination device and set it in front of you. If it is sitting on the sigil, that's fine. If you're using a pendulum, draw an equal armed cross on the paper. For the vertical line write YES, for the horizontal line write NO. Invoke Astaroth over these items as well, then say:

"Ashtaroth - Let me see clearly and show me which choice Is best for me."

Present each choice one by one and use the divination device on each one. Ashtaroth invoked before divination brings stronger, clearer images and insight, and more forthright answers.

When finished, Thank Ashtaroth. You may keep the sigil for future divination sessions. Some people, especially those who work divination often, may choose to make this sigil of a more permanent material like wood or clay, or even glass or stone.

CHAPTER 3
SEVEN IMPORTANT POINTS

Now that we've discussed expectations, planning, and opportunity, let's look at the various ingredients to a person's success. Successful people have several traits in common that those who seek success should strive to cultivate in themselves. So most importantly, successful people are disciplined. They get the job done. They don't think it to death - they're motivated to do something about their passion. Because of this, they often cultivate discipline. They are dedicated to their work. That means that their ideas don't just sit on the back burner forever. Most successful people actually have a real-world talent. Whether that talent is being able to negotiate deals, or to inspire others, or an ability to sell expensive purses - they have some kind of talent. So, when I say talent, it's not always a "creative" talent that I mean. These people also have magickal talent even if they are not magicians. How so? Magickal talent in that they know how to manipulate situations to their own benefit, thus causing change that conforms to their own will. Finally, many of them, certainly not all, have money management skills which is a key component when we're talking about having lasting prosperity and wealth. They also possess some self-confidence, or at least confidence in their ideas or talents.

So, to recap - wealth/prosperity magick, aside from planning and opportunity, relies on seven important points:

1. Discipline and dedication
2. Passion
3. Motivation
4. Magickal Talent
5. Actual Real-World Talent
6. Confidence in themselves
7. Money Management Skills

In the next seven chapters of this book, we're going to hit each one of these topics. For those who just said, "Screw the first fifteen chapters of this book, I'm going straight to chapter sixteen for the good stuff!" I wish them the best of luck. But for those of you who are still reading, I expect you're going to go far. Your prosperity magick will likely be longer lasting and life-long. After all, it's not like Daemons are magickal genii who will grant you three wishes. If they were, I wouldn't be writing this book because no one would need it.

CHAPTER 4
DISCIPLINE AND DEDICATION

Discipline is the driving force behind the meat of success. Some might argue it's timing or luck, and while those may sometimes be factors at play, timing and luck aren't always controllable elements in success. Those you can leave to the Daemonic. But discipline is something you can control. By discipline I don't mean you have to lose your sense of humor and start wearing a suit. What I do mean is you need to devote time every day to achieving your goals. If you want to be an all-star athlete, that means getting up every morning and practicing your sport. If you are seeking a career as a singer, that means you have to get up every day and practice. If you're a painter, you should paint every day. If you're an Egyptologist, you should get up every day and study or head to Egypt to dig up artifacts or see the artifacts in person. You get the picture.

You also don't get to skip a day or slack. That doesn't mean you can't have vacations or weekends off, but it does mean you should be dedicated to what you're doing and schedule your time accordingly. If you want something bad enough - you're going to make time for it. **If you refuse to make time for it - you didn't want it bad enough.**

Discipline and dedication often means keeping a schedule. Studies have shown most successful people keep a day planner or some type of written schedule that they stick to. This means that every morning or once a week you need to sit down and plan your road to success by setting aside blocks of time to work. Perhaps some of that time is spent in production, part of it is spent marketing, and part of it is spent answering email. It also means learning how to limit distractions to keep yourself on schedule.

The schedule works much like the goal list, and mastering the schedule takes a bit of trial and error. The schedule itself boosts productivity and keeps you on task during your journey to success.

When you initially begin your schedule, if you have a clear plan where you're going, you can start with the year, highlighting deadline days where there are tasks you expect to have completed. Then you work your way down to scheduling out the month, and then the week, and finally each individual day. Knowing clearly where you're going and how long each task will take goes a long way to making the schedule work. But you also need to learn to be flexible. Leave a little wiggle room in the schedule because things come up and can derail a perfectly planned day.

Your Agenda vs. Other People's Agendas

One of the biggest issues people have when they start scheduling is learning to put their own agenda over the agendas of others. Even I still struggle with this at times. Random phone calls, friends stopping by, and even email can cause you to lose focus of your own agenda and send you off on someone else's. I'm not saying you need to be selfish, but there are a few things you can do to limit the derailing effects of other people's agendas. Other people's agendas are distractions, and unless someone else is in immediate danger of dying (or they're deathly ill or some such thing), any want for your time during your working hours is a no-no. You need to learn to say no to those people. Distractions come in all kinds of flavors and the successful person knows how to limit them.

Motivational speaker Brandon Buchard is famously known for saying: *"Beware your inbox. It is nothing but a convenient organizing system for other people's agendas."*

In this he means that oftentimes those seeking to bring success on themselves get sidetracked with crap that could easily be put off until later. One of those things we can often put off is email. Schedule time every day to answer your email and try to avoid looking at it first thing in the morning.

Instead, have your coffee, get your exercise in, and start your day. Only then should you look at email and categorize it into two different folders. The first folder is YOUR AGENDA. These are emails you want to respond to quickly because they will further your agenda. The second folder is THEIR AGENDA. These are emails that don't need to be answered right now because they aren't helping you. They're helping someone else. And unless your job is customer service based, those emails don't further YOUR agenda. So, Aunt Margaret's invitation to little Billy's birthday party can wait. But your customer's inquiry into buying bulk widgets from you IS important because that brings in the money and pays the bills. It contributes to your success in creating your widget building business. For authors, emails containing praise, criticism, or questions about a book can wait a few days. But emails from editors or cover artists should be answered in a timely manner. So, based on your business, some email can wait, while the rest should be dealt with immediately. Choose one day a week to answer other people's agendas, but clear your email of those things that further your agenda 1-2 times a day. It really depends on your volume. Otherwise you could spend hours upon hours dealing with email and getting nothing else done.

There are a lot of other types of distractions. Like phone calls. Try to schedule them, otherwise, make people leave a message and get back to them at another time. Unless, of course, your business relies on customer service, in which case it may be in your best interest to take calls as they come in. Remember that for every interruption to your work day, it will take fifteen minutes for you to get back to what you were doing. You'd be amazed at how much you can get done when you limit these types of distractions.

For those of you who run home-based businesses or who are self-employed, another type of distraction are the family members and friends who think because you work out of your house, that you can take off and do whatever you want when you want to. You become the person they call when little Johnny gets sick at school because, well, "It's easier for you to stop whatever you're doing and go pick him up from school than it is for me." Or they may ask you to have lunch with them a few times a week. Or because they're not working, they assume that since you're home - you aren't working either. This can be especially detrimental to those who work creative jobs including musicians, computer programmers, artists, and writers. You have to draw a line in the sand with your loved ones and tell them that your work time is still your work time. I have literally turned off the phones and all messaging during my work time. If it's an emergency, my close family and friends know how to break through and get in contact with me. Make sure yours do, too.

Next - one of the biggest time sucks in our modern age is the Internet and social media. A lot of people were upset when, back in 2010 I decided to remove myself from all of the online occult forums I belonged to and decided to spend my time getting serious about my writing career. How many of you reading this spend more time online chatting and minding everyone else's business instead of minding your own? We've all been guilty of it. Sure, it can be a nice way to relax and unwind after a long day, but you need to learn to limit your time online. Being online can be addictive. It fills our need for instant gratification whether it be how many likes we get on a post, or having a wonderful group of friends on a forum. It's tempting to see if those friends have responded to our latest comment or observation. It's validating to get feedback. But when being online keeps you from getting anything meaningful done, then is it serving you? I'm not saying you should dump your social media and stay off the Internet, but when it comes to your own success in following your goals and reaching your dreams, you do have to ask yourself if you're spending too much time on the internet. If so, limit your time. Use an alarm to tell you when to get offline, or install a program on your computer that limits your ability to visit those time-sucking sites during your work time. You may find not being a slave to social media is liberating and allows you to get more done to make your life better!

Finally, you have to sit down and work whether you want to or not. The road to success is paved with doing all kinds of crap you hate. Even the thing you love to do has shitty jobs attached to it. For example - being in business for yourself brings with it bookkeeping chores whether you like them or not. They're there. I loved working in accounting for all those years because I enjoy working with numbers. Numbers are consistent. But with those numbers came both nice and cranky customers. Sometimes you have to deal with the cranky customers. It's the nature of the beast. There's always going to be that one task you hate, or those moments where you feel uninspired or blocked from getting things done. You have to learn how to navigate those blocks and keep working in spite of them.

One last thing — if you define prosperity in family and friends - be sure to make time for them too. It's okay to slip lunch with your sister into your schedule. Or family time. These things are important to our well-being. It's not about all work and no play. It's about making time for the things that matter to further your sense of prosperity and well-being in **all** aspects of your life.

Bael's Creative Unblocking Spell

I once asked my friend whose coven's patron is Ba'al what the difference between Bael and Ba'al was. His answer: *one letter and an apostrophe*. Many Daemonolaters believe these variant spellings are either mistakes in how the grimoires and Daemonic names were copied down, or done on purpose to invoke a different aspect of the same Daemonic force.

In this case, I am saying Bael instead of Ba'al because the variant spelling, for me, brings about a different aspect of Ba'al. That is, the creative aspect. For me, Bael is a Daemon of creators. A muse of sorts. He brings a creative fire to the imagination and sets it free.

Now the fun part -- this is a channeling ritual filled with automatic writing wherein hopefully you'll get some good stuff. It's meant to unleash your muse and get your creative juices flowing. I actually avoided putting this ritual into the book until the very end just because I debated including it. For those who suffer from ADHD or similar maladies, this ritual can cause a bit of chaos. Afterward you may want to do all the things Bael (and your own internal Daemons) want in one shot, and become so overwhelmed you get nothing done it all. So, the key is to focus and concentrate on Bael, and allowed him to give you as many ideas as he sees fit. But once the ritual is over, pick one idea and focus on that. You can always go back to the others. The hard part is going to be taking the one that you love the most and focusing on that while the other wonderful ideas are just sitting there waiting. I know – I struggle with this, too! For those of you who are creative, you completely understand where I'm coming from. I see you smirking right now.

Make sure you have a pen and pad of paper. Having a skill for channeling is imperative for this. As much as I hate to say it, if you have no skills in the psychic department, whether it be clairvoyance, clairaudience, or clairsentience - you're not going to get nearly as much from working with the Daemonic divine as those who do. This is sometimes why in the old grimoires there was both an operator and a seer. Many of the rituals that I put my books are for the seer/operator because many magicians are expected to do both. If you are not a seer, or do not possess the necessary psychic skills, you might seek out a magickal partner who is a seer and work the rituals together.

You Need:

- one lamen of Bael (A lamen is a type of magickal pendant and in this case, it is a symbolic representation of the magician's relationship to Bael and is used as a focal point for the work.)
- a pad of paper
- a pen

You can do this ritual within an elemental circle, or ritual construct of your own choice. If not, directly invoke the Daemon using his Enn: *Ayer Secore On Ca Ba'al (or Bael)*

Now imagine yourself alone in the room when, from the South East, you see a figure. His dark shadowy figure comes toward you. Whisper his Enn again (committing it to memory helps a bit here). Now imagine the Daemon touching you. Concentrate on feeling his energy. Allow him to merge with you. As you feel the merge, breathe into it, surrender to it. Once the merging is complete, take up the lamen of Bael and put it around your neck, then pick up the pen and tablet. Close your eyes again and breathe in, setting pen to paper.

Ask the Daemon to work through you to create. Then open up and let what comes next happen. I can't tell you what will end up on your pad of paper. I've received drawings, entire chapters of books, outlines, and lists of things. Others I know who perform this type of ritual work have ended up with detailed schematics, pictures, and even recipes or formulas.

There is no set time on these sessions, though I recommend that you end the session once you begin to feel fatigue. Don't forget to thank Bael for his attention and help. Being in such close contact with the Daemonic like this can take its toll on the human body. Afterward, you may even feel like resting. Others will feel energetic and unable to concentrate. I can't tell you which reaction you'll have. But you will have one. It's very rare that a Daemonic force doesn't react with our own subtle bodies with prolonged contact. So, give yourself time to rest, or "come down" before trying to take on any creative endeavor, otherwise you could inadvertently burn yourself out.

Orobas' Smooth Transition Talisman

This little talisman packs a big punch when you've got big things going on in your life and need a smooth transition.

Using clay or wood, carve, draw, or burn the following sigil onto the talisman, all the while saying Orobas' Enn: *Jedan tasa hoet naca Orobas*

If clay, bake it as needed. If you are turning this into a wearable talisman, be sure to drill the holes necessary, insert jump rings, etc… Once you have the completed talisman, take it into meditation with you. Before you start each meditation invoke Orobas using the Enn above, then begin to infuse the talisman with calm, smooth transitional energy. While holding it, think calming thoughts, and think of carefree days. If it helps, you can play sounds of nature or water in the background. Focus on the present moment or the breath. At the end of the meditation, say the Enn again, and then thank Orobas for his influence.

Do this meditation over the talisman for thirty minutes for seven days. After that, you can wear the talisman during the transition and it should have the effect of calming you and helping situations run more smoothly. This talisman can be recharged and worn over the long-term, or as needed.

On the color of the clay: Consider using blue or gray. These are calming colors, and since the point of this talisman is smooth transition, calming colors work best.

Problem Solving Meditation

First, this meditation requires no Daemons. Just a pen and a piece of paper. This is something I learned from my first magickal mentor many years ago and it's been a valuable tool in my magician's toolbox for a long time. It will help relax the mind and open up your problem-solving capabilities. Sometimes what we need to do is look at a problem from a different angle. We need perspective.

On a piece of paper, draw the following simple spiral.

Imagine your problem sitting at the center of the spiral. Now, with your eyes, focus on the lines and follow them around and around to the center, then back out again. Back in, back out. Do this three times and feel yourself relax as you do it. Then focus on the problem at the center of the spiral. Imagine the problem working its way out of the spiral maze until it's all the way out and standing alongside the spiral. You probably have an image in your mind of what the problem looks like. Could be a square, could be the shape of a car or an arrow. Whatever it is, draw the problem (a pictorial representation) to the right of the spiral. Now pick up the paper and turn it 45 degrees and look at both images. Turn it another 45 degrees and look again. Do this until you've examined the images from all sides. Now close your eyes and relax. Ask yourself the following questions:

> What am I not seeing?
> How can I make things work in my favor?
> What is my best course of action?

Now just sit quietly and listen. Pay attention closely. If thoughts come and go, just observe them and allow them to float by. Don't react to them. Let them come and go like waves. After about fifteen minutes of this, stop and go about your day/night. If you got nothing during the meditation – that's fine. That night before bed, take a warm shower or bath, get comfortable, and sleep. Allow a good night's sleep to refresh you and lend insight. By the following morning you'll have gained perspective.

Sometimes this ritual reveals what you thought was a problem wasn't really a problem. Or it wasn't as big of a problem as you made it out to be. Other times it will show you things you didn't see before, thus leading to a course for correction.

CHAPTER 5
PASSION

Passion is the key to perseverance. You would think it would be discipline, but the reality is that without passion you would have no need to persevere. You have to love what you do in order to be successful at it. Like I mentioned in the last chapter, there will always be parts of your career you hate. That's inevitable, but there has to be something about it that you love. Now is not the time to lie to yourself about what you love. If what you love about your job is the people, the numbers, the problem solving — figure out what it is because THAT is your key to success. You can be good at something all day long, but unless you really love it, you haven't taken it to the next level where success is possible.

You've heard the phrase *play to your strengths*? Well, there is a great deal of strength in passion. Passion motivates us toward discipline and dedication to something.

To help better discover those things you're passionate about, try the following:

In a notebook, write down all the activities you love. Then write down what you love about them. For example, if you love roller coasters, you may love them for the adrenaline rush you get from the fear you feel as the cart races down a steep hill at eighty-plus miles per hour. While another person may love them for their architecture and design. Same love - different reasons. Never assume people love the same things you love for the exact same reasons. If you love numbers because you love problem solving, that might lead you to becoming a mathematician or a math teacher. But if you love numbers because big ones excite you and you like the fact that they're consistent and don't lie, you may choose to become an accountant or a stock broker. If you like people and interacting with them and being social, you may gravitate toward a career in hospitality or a service industry where customer service is key. Or you may like helping people, so you go into nursing. Or, if you just like trying to figure out what makes them tick - psychology or counseling. Social people often do well in sales and marketing, too.

If you love a certain subject, you might consider going into teaching or research. The possibilities are endless here. To find our strengths we really need to examine all those things we're passionate about. Remember the story of my friend who loved dogs and writing, and how she turned both of her passions into a profitable, successful career of both writing books, training dogs, and being a leading animal behaviorist? There you go. If your success is defined by your career - then this is how you should approach it.

What if your success is defined by family and friends though? What then? You can still be passionate about raising your children, or filling your life with friends and family. You just need to make life choices that align with this. If you want to be successful at your home-based business because you want to have more time for your family and friends, then it's still in your best interest to do a job you love.

Of course, if your passion includes not having a job, then perhaps it's your view toward work that needs to change. Some people live to work. Others work to live. And others still say that if you do something you love for a living, you'll never work a day in your life. I contest the latter simply because life is full of messy chores no one wants to do. Like scrub the toilet or clean out the ferret cage. I have yet to meet a person who loves all of life's chores. Yet I have met people who started their own cleaning business because they love to clean, and it gives them gratification to do it. There will always be people who love to fix things and get their hands dirty. There will always be people who want to spend their lives surrounded by children.

You've heard someone, at some point in your life, say, *"He really missed his calling…"* when they run across someone who is good at one thing, but instead is doing something completely counterintuitive with his life, right? What would others say your calling is? I have a family member who is great with kids. She loves being around kids. She enjoys watching kid movies. She works as a manager right now. We often say she missed her calling working with children. She would have made a fantastic teacher or nanny, and she likely would have been much happier in a career involving children.

Right now, I want you to either ask your partner, or your friends and family, what THEY think you're good at. There are two sides to you. The side you know, and the side everyone else sees. What do other people envision are your passions? If someone was to peg the calling you missed, what would they say? Finally - do you agree? (This is also a question to ask others, and yourself about your strengths.)

Asmodai Rite to Find Your Passion

This is a ritual for creativity or call to action. It can be performed when you feel dead inside, unmotivated, or uninspired.

In the ritual space place three red candles in a straight line about 1-3 feet from each other. If you're working on carpet, get yourself several pieces of wood to put the candles on (for stability) or use tables.

Invoke Asmoday, Asmodeous, and Amducious as follows.

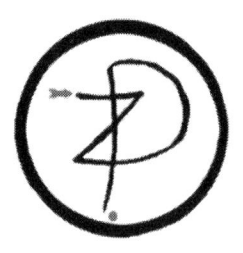

At the first candle, use the ZD sigil to invoke Asmoday by employing the Enn, "*Alan Typan Asmoday*". Light the candle.

Go to the second candle and invoke, "*An Ayer on ca Asmodeus*!" Light the candle.

Go to the third candle and invoke, "*Secore myasa icar Amducious*!" Light the candle.

Go back to the first candle and lift your hands above your head. "*I seek inspiration! I seek to find my passion!*" Bring your hands to your temples. "*This is to see!*"

Go to the second candle and lift your hands above your head and declare, "*I seek passion!*" Bring your hands to your heart and say, *"This is to feel!"*

Go to the third candle and lift your hands above your head and say, *"I seek action!"* Bring your hands to your sides and say, *"This is to move!"*

Circle the candles three times clockwise. During each round chant, *"By Asmoday, Asmodeus, and Amducious may the fire within ignite! Show me my passion!"*

Finally, write on a piece of parchment what you think your passion is. If you don't know, then just write your name on the paper and then burn it in the offering bowl. Close the ritual.

Repeat this for three nights. Some report having dreams showing them what their passion is, while others report being given a sign within a week of concluding the ritual. I find this ritual helpful to bring back inspiration when I'm feeling down and uninspired. It works in both instances.

Chapter 6
Motivation

Confidence can play a huge role in our motivation. When we work with our talents and passions, we become more confident in what we're doing. The more confident we are, the more motivated we feel. Nonetheless, motivation can be a fickle thing. Not everyone will be motivated by the same thing. Some people are self-motivated, while others need a gentle push from their loved ones or someone who believes in them. Others are only motivated by reward, and the higher the reward, the more the motivation.

In a journal, I want you to explore the things that motivate you toward your passion. Is it money? The promise of more free time? A solid ego stroke? Or maybe you're motivated by survival alone. There's nothing wrong with that unless you're terribly unhappy.

Once you figure out all of the things that motivate you, some people find it helpful to create a reward system. In this sense, they know that getting things done will trigger a reward response. Much like experiments, such as Pavlov's dogs, humans can condition themselves to productivity by rewarding themselves when tasks are complete.

The fact is that you cannot have prosperity without being motivated to work toward that prosperity. The goal of many magickal exercises is to change the way we think about a situation, thus changing the situation itself. I know, it sounds like a bunch of *new age* nonsense. The truth remains that many studies have been done that show that people who have a positive outlook tend to be more successful overall. This requires striking the words "I can't" from our vocabulary, as well as many other negative things that we tell ourselves.

Motivation can be a fickle thing because sometimes we look for excuses to not complete a task or project. Writers, for example, will often use house chores as an excuse as to why they don't have time to write. I repeat again - if something is important, you will make time for it. If your prosperity is important to you, you will make time for it. Since each individual's definition of prosperity is unique, that has to be taken into account as well.

Motivation killers include procrastination, excuses, and negative self-talk. I'm sure there are many other barriers to motivation that can plague us as well, like a soul sucking day job that leaves you feeling mentally fried at the end of your day. When one has a job like that, one of the last things we want to do when we get home from work is to sit down and spend hours working on a goal or dream – even if it may lead to our eventual prosperity.

Sometimes the magick is in circumventing the self-sabotaging things we do or tell ourselves. This is why just doing the spell for money may produce a short windfall, but never lasting prosperity. We need to magickally work on those individual issues that are actually holding us back.

Your job as a magician is to do the path work that will identify these issues so that you can attack them one by one. Let me put this into context with an example scenario. Let's say you aspire to be wealthy. As has been brought up already, there needs to be a genuine path to wealth. Unless you come from a wealthy family where you stand to inherit millions when someone else passes on and passes that legacy to you, many of us do not have such opportunities for wealth. This means we must carve our own path to financial prosperity. So, the first thing you need to do is figure out by what means will you gain wealth? Usually people ask me, "Can't the Daemons just give me wealth?" We can leave this up to them, but this usually results in windfalls of money. Maybe a few thousand won in a lottery, or one of our relatives dies and leaves us twenty thousand dollars. Alternatively, the Daemons can have twisted senses of humor and you may end up in a terrible accident that leaves you paralyzed. So maybe a lawsuit will win you millions of dollars, but at that point you're stuck in a wheelchair and I imagine that's not quite how you were thinking you would become wealthy. By having a firm path to prosperity, you don't give magick room to improvise, whether you're working with Daemons, gods, angels, or other natural forces.

The point is to release water from the dam of prosperity, and to not let it sweep you away. Instead you want to allow yourself to go with the current in a controlled way. The more prepared you are, and the clearer your path, the easier it is to steer. So, by what means will you gain wealth? Once you have this path planned, this is where motivation comes in. It's not just motivation to actually work the magick and to do the internal work required to put yourself in that mindset for financial prosperity, but the motivation to do the work to get you from where you are to that point of prosperity that you aspire to.

The problem with a lack of motivation is that it impedes our progress toward that final goal. That said there are many magickal tools and techniques we can use to help spur that productivity and our motivation.

A Standard Motivation Rite

Stuck in a pattern of procrastination? This ritual will get your motivation running again. Of course, you first have to be motivated enough to do the ritual, right?

You Need:

- 6 Red Candles
- Parchment
- Writing device
- 1-2 Drops of Blood

First, take six red or orange candles (symbolic of fire) and place one at each directional point of your ritual space and two on your altar. Light them. From the South invoke Flereous using his Enn, *Ganic Tasa Fubin Flereous*. From the East invoke Amducious *Denyen valocur avage secore Amducious*, from the North invoke Amon *Avage Secore Ammon ninan*, and from the West invoke Agares *Rean ganen ayar da Agares*. Above the altar invoke Abigor, *Aylan Abigor tasa uan on ca*.

On the parchment write down all the things you'd do with motivation. Seal with your blood, and burn in the offering bowl.

Chapter 7
Magickal Talent

Magickal talent comes in a variety of manifestations. Some people are good at energy work, some people are good at grounding energy. Others excel at weather working and others do well with divination. Magickal talent varies from person to person and just like skills like sewing or cooking, you can actually learn most magickal skills with a great deal of practice. There may be a few exceptions to this rule, but for the most part - you can learn to manifest and grow your talents.

Having some magickal talent can go a long way to helping you meet your goals. As the old axiom says, *"If at first you don't succeed, try, try again!"* Persistence is important when seeking to gain mastery (or at least competence and proficiency) of any skill. This includes manifesting prosperity in your life. Manifesting prosperity is never as easy as saying an incantation, drawing a sigil, and poof - instant success. If it were that easy, more magicians would be prosperous in every area of their lives. Even prosperity takes practice, and the magick used to draw that prosperity requires tweaks and adjustments along the way until you hit on the thing that works for you.

One of the stories I like to tell when it comes to developing magickal talent is a story about a young woman who contacted me a few years ago who was interested in learning to communicate with the Daemonic like I do. She coveted my skills. I'm not sure what she was expecting. Perhaps she was expecting a magic pill, or simple ritual, that would give her the skills overnight. Unfortunately, all I could give her were the exercises in *Drawing Down Belial*. I assured her that by practicing these exercises daily, she would increase her magickal talent for Daemonic communication. Three days later she contacted me to let me know she had not gotten any results. She told me she was frustrated.

Basically, in this entire book I've been telling you that a strong work ethic is an essential ingredient to prosperity. That goes for everything in life, not just wealth. Anything worth doing is worth doing well. If it's important to you, it's even more important for you to have a strong work ethic.

The woman in this story likely never did hone her Daemonic communication skills. She wanted instant gratification, or some quick way to gain the skills that I have worked over thirty years to master. The point being that if you really seek to hone the magickal skills that will help your magick manifest, you will make time to practice those skills. If you cannot be bothered to practice or work toward a specific goal, the only person you hurt is yourself. If you really seek to be prosperous and you feel that one of the things holding you back is your lack of magickal skill, then you need a clear path to increase those skills by using them. You can read all the books you want and learn everything possible about the skills you're trying to improve, but until you actually put those skills into practice on a regular basis, you cannot hope to increase that skill or achieve mastery. This goes for any skill. Not just magickal talent. Never once have I met someone who has studied woodworking, for example, and read every book out there on the subject, who sat down for the first time able to produce artisan crafts from wood. It takes years and years of working with the wood, of using the tools, and practicing one's technique before one becomes a master woodcarver. It works the same way with magick.

I would include spells and rituals in this section as well, for gaining skill, however the skills each of us need to work on are likely different. I encourage each of you to make an honest assessment of your magickal skills, and then find resources to help you build those skills. I do recommend that every magician pause every now and again and go back to the beginning. Sometimes when we go back to the beginning with fresh eyes, we see a lot of the things we missed the first time around. So, if for example, you are unable to practice successful invocation, go back to the beginning and find out what you missed. Then go forward with that knowledge to practice in those areas where you feel you are not strong enough. I recommend a minimum of two hours a week devoted to any particular magickal skill.

In that rare instance where at least one year of regular practice has gone by and your skill has not increased, I recommend you try a different approach. Someone who has no skill for clairvoyance may never be able to learn how to scry. There are many ways around the wall - you just need to find it. I should probably point out that when I say regular practice, I mean daily, or in the very least weekly. If you do not have time for this then I question how badly you really want it. If you want something bad enough you will make time for it. It's all about priorities. When you begin making your prosperity a priority, you are that much closer to achieving your goals.

Chapter 8
Real-World Talent

Talent doesn't just flow innately from anyone. Talents may be something you have a natural aptitude for, but they often include skills that require practice for development. This is where discipline comes in. How hard are you willing to work to hone your talents and turn them into something that draws opportunity and prosperity to you?

See, Daemons can't work with nothing. You need to give them something to work with. You can draw up all the pacts and do all the magick spells out there to become a(n) [insert awesome career title], but the fact of the matter is that if you do not have talent or experience in that awesome career field, it's not going to manifest.

"But I don't have any talents," you might be complaining right now.

Everyone has a talent. I don't care who you are, there is something you excel at in life, even if it is serving as a bad example. I bring this up because I have met a lot of people who have made a lot of bad decisions, who turned around and used those bad decisions to educate others in how not to make bad decisions. That, right there, takes some talent.

You need to think outside the box if you don't feel you have a talent.

The following bears repeating here because it may help your perspective. In magick, perspective is everything. In the book *Sex, Money and Power*, I asked readers to do the following exercise:

Open up a notebook and on the first available five pages, I want you to label the first page TRAITS. On the second write TALENTS. On the third write SKILLS. On the fourth write JOBS. Finally, on the fifth page, write JOBS I WANT.

TRAITS: On the first page - I want you to write down all of your strongest traits. Now is NOT the time to be humble. Are you funny? Do you have a commanding presence? If you're not book smart - do you possess street smarts?

TALENTS: Next let's write down all of your talents! If you can sing like a bird, write it down! Do you draw cool comics? Write it down. Are you good with numbers or making things grow? Write that down, too! Write down everything you're really good at, even if it's being nice to people. Everyone – EVERYONE, has talents.

SKILLS: Next - write down all of your skills. Did you learn farming from your grandfather? Did your dad teach you how to fish? Maybe you're incredible with a sewing machine. Did you learn typing? Perhaps you're really good with computers or you play an instrument.

JOBS: Now write down the jobs you've had or currently hold.

JOBS YOU WANT: Keeping in mind your traits, talents, and skills - write down jobs you'd like to have. For example, someone who is shy, skilled with numbers, and who can write really well likely won't do well as a famous singer (especially if you can't sing), but you might be able to work as a songwriter, publicist, agent, or manager in the realm of music. That is unless you are prepared to conquer your shyness and learn to sing.

Next - make a list of all the reasons you don't have the job you want.

If you do have the job you want -- write down why it's not bringing you the wealth and prosperity you expect it should be.

Note all the reasons (excuses vs. the legitimate reasons) that you're not working in a field you love, or one that is more financially lucrative. What steps can you take to get a better job or get a job you think you'll love?

Now ask yourself the million-dollar question -- do you really want wealth, or would you just like to be comfortable doing what you love? A lot of people THINK they want to be filthy rich when they'd be perfectly happy with a job they enjoy and enough money to live their lives in relative comfort.

The exercise you did in chapter five also applies here. If you didn't do it, do it now. Ask your loved ones and those close to you what they think your biggest strengths and talents are. Ask them what calling they think you missed. Do you agree? If not, why?

Finally - ask yourself the honest question — Do I have the talents and skills I need to move forward and begin my prosperous journey? If not, how can you get them? What actionable steps can you take to get the skills you need, or hone the talents you have?

A Final word - This is a perfect exercise to do if you are considering a career change, or you're hitting that midlife crisis and questioning your career choice before now.

Leviathan's I Dream of Talent Spell

This is a very simple ritual that doesn't require a lot of preparation or set up, or even time. On a piece of parchment or a plain piece of paper, draw the sigil of Leviathan first thing in the morning. For the entire day, carry the sigil with you whether you keep it in your purse, wallet, or pocket. Several times throughout the day allow yourself a few moments to look at the sigil and ask yourself what your talents are. Before bed in the evening, pull out the sigil and ask again what your talents are. Whisper over the sigil the Enn of Leviathan: *Jaden Tasa Hoet Naca Leviathan*.

Now place the sigil beneath your mattress and go to bed. Repeat this as needed.

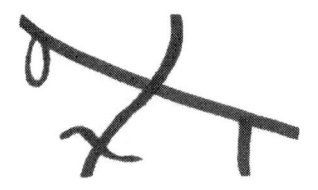

The results should be that you dream of your talents and strengths. Leviathan reveals truths about ourselves, even if we're in denial about them. So maybe you'll never be a great dancer, but if you dream of adding numbers on a calculator, perhaps you're better suited to a career in finance. Be sure to keep a notebook, voice recorder, or your phone handy by the side of the bed so you can note anything you remember from the dreams. Leviathan often brings very vivid dreams that are easily remembered. Of course, results will vary based on the magician and their personal skills. Those who are more psychic are more apt to remember the dreams and get the most from this type of ritual.

Clauneck's Career Counseling Rite

You may be laughing your ass off at the idea of Clauneck as your career counselor, but I want you to hold that image in your mind for a moment because that's exactly what's going to happen. Except it won't be a guy in the suit, or a sweater vest, with glasses, giving you advice. Clauneck will be the disembodied two-by-four-of-reality hurling toward your head. **Warning:** This rite may result in shock or hurt feelings.

In this aspect, Clauneck is more of a wise father figure giving you a solid assessment in the form of judging you and then telling you exactly what he thinks. He's not going to hold back. In this case the advice and judgment just happens to be about your career. You should have heard what my father said about my career - I think he and Clauneck share a few traits there.

Don't worry, Clauneck's not going to make you fill out any forms or career assessment tests, but he may give you real-world tests in the form of opportunities or obstacles. With opportunities, the point would be to get you to try out different things to help you find a career that suits you. A lot of people think that they might like one career or another, but then they get into that career and discover it wasn't everything they thought it would be. This is why you meet so many people who have a degree in one thing, but are working in a completely different field twenty years later. Sure, sometimes it's because there isn't money (or jobs) in the field that they originally went to school for. But many times, it's because they found that the career they thought they wanted, wasn't what they thought it was.

I use writing in a lot of examples because that is my profession. So, for example, with writers, a lot of people want to be writers, but then they sit down to write that first book and discover that while they may be able to tell stories and write pretty well, they don't have the attention span or discipline to finish a book. Some people discover they can't handle the loneliness you have to endure to be a writer. These are the types of things we don't think of when we're choosing our dream career. We're thinking of the parts we think we'll enjoy. The book signings, the doting fans, the potential movie deal. We're thinking of the Stephen Kings of the world when we get into careers like this, despite people reminding us that super successful novelists amount to maybe one percent of the writing population. We also don't see the hours of time spent alone, slaving over a manuscript. We just see the extroverted writer persona doing interviews, chatting away on social media, and signing books. We always know that when we get into our dream career, we will be among the exceptions.

Just like some people like to bake and think they would like to open a bakery, but they don't realize that they have to get up at three o'clock in the morning in order to be open by seven AM with fresh baked goods ready to go. Someone may enjoy playing music with their band, but discover that going on tour, and being away from home so much, wasn't anything they expected (or wanted). Because of these unexpected twists and turns in these various careers, some people who otherwise would be very good in these careers, find they can't deal with a certain aspect of it. So, they change their path. Does that mean you still can't have some type of career that harnesses your passion? Of course not. You may just need to find a different road to your success in that career, or find your angle.

Maybe you would be better off in a career as a studio musician, or with a band that only plays locally, instead of traveling all the time. Maybe instead of writing novels, your talent is in short stories, or writing articles for webzines or news sites. As always, sound money management, good business and financial decisions, and plenty of planning will go a long way to making things work in your favor.

But for now, let's concentrate on getting Clauneck's help in choosing a career that harnesses your skills and passions, and consists of tasks you can effectively manage without feeling like you're in over your head. Don't be surprised if he doesn't show you a few things you didn't want to see while he's at it. He's not going to be nice. If you want to be a race car driver and he tells you that your driving sucks and needs significant improvement for that to happen - that's the truth of it. If he thinks your writing sucks, or you can't sing to save your life - he's going to tell you that. By no means should you take this as a sign to give up on your dream. He's just saying there needs to be significant improvement, so you would need to learn to drive better, or take some writing classes, or hire a singing coach. He's going to tell you what you have to do to "level up" so-to-speak.

After that, the choice is yours.

In your ritual space, construct an elemental circle or ritual construct of your own design. If you choose not to work within this configuration, that's fine. As with most rituals you probably want to enter your ritual space freshly bathed and purified. Though I have found that as long as you're not carrying too much negativity into the temple, you're probably fine. For those who do carry a lot of negativity, or work in negative environments, a quick shower, a few minutes dispelling negativity through meditation, and drinking a cup of water usually does the trick.

Clauneck can be invoked from the North, Northeast, or East. For this particular ritual, I would invoke from the Northeast of the ritual chamber. Begin by saying his invocation: *Evna ana se nac Clauneck.*

Drawing in a deep breath, say, *"Clauneck I seek your aid. I ask that through your wisdom you show me the path to my prosperity and success. I accept your judgment and assessment, and most importantly your advice. I will give my due diligence to take your wisdom under advisement."*

After saying these words, close your eyes and imagine a silver light surrounding you. Whisper the invocation a second time, take a deep breath, exhale, and listen. There's a reason you're not sitting down for this, and it's because you want the demon to know that you are willing to stand up and take responsibility for all that you are. Clauneck does not want practitioners to sit on bended knee before him begging for money or prosperity. The magician must stand proud and unmoving in the face of Clauneck.

What will be revealed to you during this time is between you and the Daemon. After about ten minutes you should be able to then sit in meditation to contemplate the thoughts and images that you have received. When you're finished, thank Clauneck for his counsel and depart the ritual chamber.

During this ritual you can carry his seal with you, but I've found it is unnecessary if you are using his Enn as the invocation.

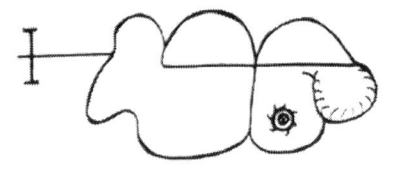

CHAPTER 9
DEDICATION

You're going to find a lot of things I talk about in this book are somewhat repetitive because they all interrelate. For example, dedication leads us back to our priorities, and our work ethic. In order to use magick to become the most prosperous person you can be, you need to be dedicated to your prosperity. You need to be dedicated to working the magick toward that prosperity. Dedicated to working with those Daemons you are calling on to help you gain that prosperity. Dedication is closely linked to a person's priorities. You need to make your prosperity a priority in your life. I hear time and time again people who think that the wealthiest among us all belong to a secret society where they do pacts with the Daemons in order to gain their millions of dollars. The fact is that people who have wealth like this initially worked hard for that success. Sure, some of them were born into it and had the success of their forefathers passed on to them, but initially someone had to work for it. Again, unless you were born into the success of a relative, the chances of you gaining that success with no work is slim to none. Daemons or not.

When discussing dedication to our own prosperity, it is important to point out that there are a few things we need to consider. Sometimes being dedicated means being confident in ourselves. Confidence is a very tricky subject because I am of the firm belief that confidence, or lack thereof, is one of those things that can make or break success. It is up to each individual to feel confident enough in their skills and ideas to actually dedicate themselves to them. If you're having a hard time dedicating yourself to your own prosperity, you might need to look into your level of confidence. Sure, everything comes with its risks and we all have moments of self-doubt, but we cannot allow the self-doubt to become so crippling that it shoots our confidence to hell.

In this instance, you might consider weeding out all of the negative influences in your life. People who are unsupportive, who are always telling you that you can't do this or that, or who are just negative and always bringing you down, may need to be removed from your life.

Finally, one of the most important parts of dedication is following through. This ties into discipline as well. Dedication equals discipline plus motivation. It is time to sit down and come to terms with whether you are highly disciplined, or highly erratic. I like to compare this to two different types of writers - Plotters and Pantsers. Plotters are people who plan out their stories, and Pantsers are those who just begin writing with no clear direction. When I first began writing I was a Pantser. I would start with a few characters and throw them into an interesting situation, and then let them figure their way out of the situation on their own. This always created several problems.

First, it always took me longer to finish the story. Second, I always got caught up in the slogging middle because I didn't know where the story was going. Third, I often ended up having to go back through and make plot adjustments during the editing phase. The same thing will happen to you if you have a goal with no clear path to get there. You'll find yourself fumbling around, getting sidetracked, and it will ultimately take you longer to get where you want to go. Writers who are Plotters have a clear direction of where they're starting and where they'll end up. They may not always have a clear idea of their middle, but they have identified signposts along the way. So, your outline to get to your prosperity doesn't need to have every detail painstakingly outlined, but you should know where you're starting, what the end goal is, and have some progress points marked along the way. Another important aspect your plan should be to develop a plan B. If one road to success is not working, approach it from a different angle, or have an alternative plan in place. Things won't always work out as you expect them to. One should have an alternative plan for each of the steps in the plan as well. If for any reason things aren't working out - don't give up. Persistence is key.

Having these plans and steps are going to help you follow through. You can start now by setting small goals for yourself. Don't look at the big picture because it will be overwhelming. Take pieces and parts of the overall situation and work on one little part at a time. When I'm working on a large book, I break it down into bite-size chunks. Whether it's a chapter, or a scene, or topic, I concentrate on that one small part until it's completed, and then I mark it off the list. Then I can move to the next item on the list. You continue like this until the entire project is complete. This is what I mean by following through. You can't just start something and then drop it halfway through because you'll never complete anything, and you won't get anywhere. So always, always finish what you start. If you are dedicated enough you will follow through.

Dagon's Psychic Vampire Identification

This ritual will help you identify and draw out all those people in your life who drain your energy and leave you feeling exhausted or down on yourself.

You may be wondering why I've included this ritual at all. As mentioned in another part of this book, one of the biggest reasons many of us don't follow our passion, or seek to do our own Great Work, or give up on our own path to prosperity is often due to other people. I believe it was Sartre who said, *"Hell is other people."* There are two types of people you will run across in this world. Those who support you and cheer you on, and who will revel in your success with you. And those who will stand in your way, becoming obstacles. They do this by either trying to get your attention and suck your focus from your own goals, they're just not supportive, or they're jealous of your success and will do anything to draw your attention away from your own goals and your own life.

These people are psychic vampires. Whether intentional or not their sole purpose is to drag you down. Most of the time people like this are miserable, or have no lives or goals for themselves. **They aspire to nothing.** They're basically the metaphoric albatross around your neck.

Your goal in this ritual is to identify the psychic vampires around you, and remove them from your life. Sometimes removal of these people is difficult because they are people that we care about. You may not be able to remove every last one of them, but you can at least distance yourself from their negative, soul-sucking influence. You can choose whether or not you allow them to sap your energy and keep you from that which serves your wealth and prosperity.

For this ritual you need a scrying device. If you don't scry, you can use pendulums with a list of names (of potential vampires) or use the pendulum with a spirit board (also called a Ouija for those of you not in-the-know) so names can be spelled out. Theoretically you could use a spirit board's planchette, too, but if you do, make sure it's properly prepared. (See either *Daemonolater's Guide to Daemonic Magick* or *Drawing Down Belial* for more information.)

Begin the ritual by invoking the elemental circle. More experienced practitioners can use a ritual space construct of their own design. Experienced practitioners can also forgo any construction of the ritual space whatsoever.

Invoke Dagon with the Enn: *Ava nan ca Dagon nanay.*

"Dagon, of the abyss and the amber fields of wheat. Dragon of the infernal void. Bring forth the images (or names) of those who are crowding my path and hindering my prosperity. Show me what it feels like to be in their presence. Help me to find these obstacles and remove them! I trust your infinite wisdom, and your wisdom within me. So be it."

Take a few moments to center yourself. When you feel centered, go ahead and peer into your scrying device and wait for the images to come forth. In many instances Dagon will show you the faces of those who are standing in your way. However, if Dagon does not believe you'll be receptive to a certain image, this ritual will have certain aftereffects. Remember that part where you asked to have Dagon show you what it feels like to be in the presence of these toxic people? You will find, when you're in the presence of those toxic to you, that you will get that feeling and it will come from nowhere. It will be like a punch in the stomach.

If you are using the pendulum to go over a list of names, go one name at a time and either choose a *yes/no* sequence at the beginning, or just ask Dagon to move the pendulum horizontally over the names of potential obstacles. You may have another method for doing this, and that's fine. The idea is to pinpoint those people in your life who are causing problems for you.

When you're done with the scrying or pendulum session, thank Dagon and close the ritual.

I can't tell you what to do about these people once you identify them, because sometimes removing certain people from your life can be difficult. You may find you have difficult choices ahead of you.

Lucifuge Confidence Booster

Obviously, the point of this ritual is to help boost your confidence. As an introduction here, I'd like to tell you a story. I have a friend who worked in retail sales for many years. By the time she was thirty-two she was tired of having what she deemed "a teenager's job." See, she started working in sales when she was sixteen, then life happened, and before she knew it, she wasn't really qualified to do much else. She could've gone back to school, but at the time she had two small children and not enough hours in the day. It took both she and her husband working full-time to keep the family afloat. I told her that with so much experience in the retail business, she could easily get a managerial job. She looked at me with sad eyes and shook her head and said, "I couldn't do that. I don't know the first thing about management."

The thing was that my friend knew a great deal about retail sales. She knew all about customer service and inventory. She helped her manager close out the receipts at night and order the stock. She'd seen how performance reviews worked, and how raises were given. In some instances, she was even doing the manager's job, so she had a pretty firm grasp on what a manager did. She could easily learn to do the things she didn't know how to do. The problem was she didn't think that she had the skills that she had.

For some people, all they need is an encouraging voice to tell them, "You know what - you should give it a shot!" My friend was not one of those people who could be easily swayed with just my encouraging voice in her ear. She had been telling herself for so long that she was not worthy of a better job, that she wasn't manager material, that she never had enough confidence to apply for a managerial position – even when others told her that she could do it.

I gave her the following meditation to do for one week. I said, "Give me one week and you will be applying for that managerial position."

She laughed at me, but took the paper that I gave her, and went home. I heard nothing for a week, and on the eighth day I got a phone call. "You were right! I got it! I got it!"

Sure enough, after the fourth day of doing the meditation, she decided, "What have I got to lose?" And put in the application for the managerial position. Two days later she got an interview, and on the seventh day she accepted the job. Where is my friend today, ten years later? She now runs her own clothing store in a quiet suburb two towns north from me. This one little meditation, she often tells me, changed her life. Because she had the courage to go for that managerial position, she learned how to manage a store. From there it was only a matter of time before she ended up becoming her own boss. What did she use to finally make that leap into business ownership? You guessed it. This Lucifuge confidence booster. She calls it her secret weapon against low self-esteem.

You need:

1 sigil of Lucifuge. This can be an amulet, or it can be written on paper.

Begin the ritual by invoking the elemental circle. More experienced practitioners can use a ritual space construct of their own design. Experienced practitioners can also forgo any construction of the ritual space whatsoever.

Next, invoke Lucifuge: *Eyen tasa valocur Lucifuge Rofocal*

Much like the meditation where you drew a Daemon through you for channeling, you're going to do something similar here. Focus on the sigil of Lucifuge. Imagine a glowing with a brilliant golden light. Focus on it until you can close your eyes and envision the sigil without needing to look at it. Imagine drawing the light from the sigil into you, infusing your own energy with its strength. In this instance you are not actually channeling the demon, you are simply drawing the demon's energy into your own as a strengthener or reinforcement. Do this meditation for as long as it takes, until you feel strong and confident. Thank Lucifuge after every session.

That is the extent of the meditation, but it can be repeated as often as necessary. The real magick happens when you apply what the meditation teaches you, to your everyday life. Every time you feel yourself descending into negative self-talk, or low self-esteem, take a moment to center yourself, pause, and imagine the sigil feeding you its strength. Use that strength to overcome the negative self-talk. Use it when you need to make the bold decisions. This strength and confidence is always there for you to use when you need it.

Leviathan Depression Breaker

It happens to all of us. We find ourselves stuck in a depression where we don't feel good about ourselves or confident in our skills. Use this ritual to uplift your spirits, re-energize, and center yourself.

I'm bringing a lot of Leviathan into this book simply because Leviathan reveals truths. He also helps us evaluate our emotional strengths, weaknesses, and reactions to various things. A person's emotional state can weigh heavily on their own prosperity. When we look at earthy/fiery types of magick like prosperity magick, we cannot disregard the airy and watery components as well. We need a very balanced approach. This is why you will find Daemons in this book that have very little to do with wealth magick directly. Instead, these Daemons serve as your support staff to help you balance the other areas of your life and psyche required for prosperity work.

The one thing that many entrepreneurs suffer is depression. As a magician, it is your natural state to be a creator. To be someone who creates his own reality. Creative people often suffer some sort of depression. For those who work in artistic fields, depression is an emotionally compromising state. Many people find they cannot create when they are emotionally compromised. If you've ever suffered from writer's block, for example, this usually stems from some type of emotional compromise whether that be a fight with your spouse or best friend, or having to put your dog to sleep.

This meditation will hopefully help you rebalance yourself, and pull yourself from the depression. However, if you are suffering from clinical depression, this ritual is not an alternative to professional psychiatric help or medication. If you find you need more help than a simple ritual, please do get help from a professional.

Before you perform this ritual, perform the elemental balancing rite found in *The Complete Book of Demonolatry*, or on the website *demonolatry.org*.

Once you're feeling balanced, sit down in a dimly lit room and get comfortable. You can have Leviathan's sigil in front of you if you wish. However, the only thing you really need to do is to invoke him using his Enn: *Jedan tasa hoet naca Leviathan.*

Delve deep into a meditative state, completely aware of your breath and how your chest rises and falls with each inhale and exhale. Now focus on yourself. In your mind's eye, see yourself from the outside. You are beautiful, you're strong, and there are so many things in your life that you have to be thankful for. Start thinking of all the wonderful things that you are grateful for. For example, a roof over your head, food in your stomach, clothes on your back. Remember that there are so many other people who have it worse, and who have less. Think of the talents and skills that you have that not everyone else possesses. Think of the people who love and care about you, and how fortunate you are to have them in your life. If you are healthy, acknowledge that you are grateful for your good health. If you have a job, even if it is not ideal, be thankful that you have a job. During this entire meditation you should be focusing on those things that are going well in your life. If negative self-talk tries to butt in, shoot it down with something positive. For example: if you're thinking, "I'm thankful I have food to eat, but it would be great to have someone to share meals with…" Add to that, "I know I will find someone like that soon."

Do this meditation no less than fifteen minutes once a day for at least seven days straight. You should begin feeling better immediately, especially if your depression is mild, but if after seven days you are still depressed, you might seek counseling. In this instance you bring Leviathan into the meditation in order to see your situation more clearly. Oftentimes depression stems from the fact that we cannot see our own situations with any objectivity. We think that our lives are completely void of good things, when oftentimes the exact opposite is true.

CHAPTER 10
MONEY

This is where many people screw themselves. They never learned how to properly manage their money. This may be due to several factors. The first is we often learn by example. If our parents were never good with money, then chances are we will have difficulty managing our finances as well. If our parents were good with their money and demonstrated to us good saving skills, and a strong work ethic, we are more likely to possess those traits. Also, our current education system in the United States (and likely elsewhere in the world) does not have a curriculum to teach young people how to manage their money (or other resources). This leaves most people unprepared for life. If we're used to being poor, this can create additional issues because our first inclination when we come into larger sums of money is to immediately splurge and spend as opposed to saving or reinvesting that money into ourselves (as with continuing education), or our businesses. If we come from a background of wealth and privilege, we run a similar risk by not truly understanding the value of money, or how to save without screwing over ourselves or others.

So, let's talk about that. After all - a Daemon can help you get a better paying job, or a raise, or more customers, but if you can't manage your money -- no amount of Daemonic intervention is going to help you. I have friends who, if they won a million dollars tomorrow, they would still end up broke and neck deep in debt because they don't know how to manage their money. Let's set magick and Daemons on the back burner for awhile, and I'm going to teach you some basic money management skills.

The following chapter is basically a collection of ideas on how you can recession proof your life, get out of debt, and hopefully keep yourself out of financial trouble during already difficult times. I didn't get overly detailed. This is really simple advice that doesn't require long explanations and if more people followed it, fewer people would be in debt. What makes me qualified to write it? Let's just say that my father still jokes that I have the first nickel I ever made, and I still squeeze it now and again to see what will come out. It's not really true, of course. I'm just a super low maintenance girl and I have enough money in the bank at any given time for emergencies, layoffs, or European vacations. I've also never been so far in debt that I had to declare bankruptcy or live in my car. Why? Because I know how to manage my money, even at times in my life when I was making very little. How about you? I'm taking it that at least some of you picked up this book because you haven't been so successful at money management.

I can tell you how I do it, but it is going to require some sacrifice on your part. Religiously speaking, sacrifices are sacred offerings to the gods/Daemons or to yourself. So, no matter how you view this, remember that making sacrifices here is all part of your Great Work on the road to prosperity.

Now before you read the word sacrifice and throw this book (or your Kindle or Nook) across the room - listen up. Westerners (especially Americans) are spoiled. We want everything bigger and better. We want the big house, the big car, and five hundred pairs of shoes. We want to have our cake and eat it too. I'm not saying you can't have your cake, and I'm not saying you can't eat part of it. I'm just saying don't be greedy. Now is the time to be realistic. Everything in moderation. It's good advice for all aspects of life.

You know, back in the day, most people were lucky to have one set of clothes, one pair of shoes, and a pot to piss in. So, consider yourself lucky. There are people in other parts of the world who don't even have that in our modern era.

First Things First -- Learn to distinguish between your wants and needs.

You need food, water, clothing (since running about naked is illegal in most places) and shelter. Depending where you live, heat or air conditioning might be a need, too. Child care might be a need if you're a single parent or both parents work outside the home. Other nice things to have, that are definitely in the *need* department, include medical care and transportation, but millions of people the world over manage to live without those last two things. Anything beyond these things are pretty much wants. A want is something you don't absolutely need for survival. They're things you can save up for and take your time acquiring depending on your financial situation.

Of course, we Americans have a really skewed view of needs, too. We want the McMansion, the big car, more food than necessary to sustain us, and a huge wardrobe - and we want it NOW. We live in an instant gratification world thanks to credit cards.

A good rule of thumb is that your rent or mortgage should not be more than one-third your household income. This means if you're a single person bringing home $2500 a month, $833.33 is about where your rent should be. You could probably swing $1000 if you absolutely had to. Sadly, the reality is that $833.33 won't get you much in most parts of the U.S., so you may need a roommate to bunk up with to get that $1700 a month two bedroom apartment.

In the area of food, most people can live off of around 2,000 calories a day (around 1,400 or so if you're trying to lose a few pounds). You don't need three squares with meat every day. U.S.

portion sizes are ridiculous. Learn portion control, eat more frequent and smaller meals every day, and watch your grocery bill drop.

Also - do you really need 12 pairs of slacks, 45 shirts, and 15 pairs of shoes? This is what I mean when I talk about taking needs to excess.

The urge to *Keep Up With The Jones'* is strong with many people. Screw the Jones' anyway. Right? I know we all get those urges to keep up with our friends and have the same toys. Resist. It's often not worth it. Think for a minute. How many things have you purchased that you haven't used in a year? Maybe it's time to go through the house, gather up all that space collecting crap and have a garage sale. Or put it on Craigslist and get rid of it. At least that way you can recuperate some of that money, maybe toss it into a savings account.

ENTERTAINMENT

It continually amazes me how much American's spend to entertain themselves. Some ideas for saving money in this area:

- Wait until a movie comes out on Pay-Per-View (or your streaming/cable service) and then watch it. It's still cheaper than movie theater tickets and you'll avoid the long lines. Plus, you won't feel as bad for spending the money if the movie stinks. This doesn't mean never go to the movies again, but when I was young, I only went to the movies maybe once or twice a year (if even that).
- Check books out from the library, or get a Kindle Unlimited subscription. Admittedly books are a weakness of mine. I can sometimes read hundreds of them a year. I finally ran out of space in my house for them. Now I have a Kindle and I regularly prune my bookshelves.

- Utilize local book swaps or used bookstores. You can often get great deals and pick up twenty or thirty hours of entertainment for under ten bucks!
- If you own an e-reader - find independent authors you love and buy their books instead of the expensive commercial books. Now that I own a Kindle I read more for less! I save money when it comes to following 50 series. (Those of you who read a lot know what I mean!) Don't get me wrong, it doesn't mean I never buy books put out by the big presses. I do, I just buy fewer of them. Why? Because I can usually get two to four decent indie books for the same price of one book put out by a major publisher. You do the math.
- When getting together with friends - have a potluck and tell everyone to bring their own alcoholic beverages if they want them. That way you're not stuck having to buy all the food and drinks.
- Instead of going out to the bar, have friends over for drinks at your house. You can buy a bottle of alcohol for the cost of two drinks at a bar. You can also get twice as much beer buying it at the store and drinking it at home. (Drink responsibly).
- For you video game junkies, join one of those video game streaming or rental services and only buy games you really must have.
- Don't forget board games and cards as alternative forms of entertainment. We all own a deck of cards. Gin Rummy anyone?
- Physical activity! Getting out and going for a walk, a bike ride, or playing in the park with the kids/dog are all brilliant ways to have fun for free, and get some exercise - something most Americans are lacking.
- Instead of eating out, have a picnic, or make cooking a family affair. It's always cheaper (and often healthier) to cook from scratch.
- Stay away from book clubs, DVD clubs, subscription boxes etc... You often end up paying a higher price and getting things you'll never use, watch, or read.

FOOD

The United States is one of the most obese nations on the planet and other countries are following suit. Why? Fast food is cheap, it's plentiful (on every corner) and it's loaded with fat, sugar, and salt (among other things). It also doesn't fill us up like healthy food does, so we end up eating in excess.

- Never shop hungry. This is a golden oldie bit of advice. It's true though. Shop hungry and you'll end up with a bunch of food you don't need. This leads me to the next bit.
- Make a list and stick to it. Deviating from the list or going without a list may cause you to splurge or buy things you didn't really need. Some stores now offer a service where you do your shopping from your list online, you pay online, then you either have it delivered to you or you go to pick it up. The pick-up option is the most economical, and the money you spend having someone else shop for you (usually as much as you'd spend on a Starbucks coffee) is worth the money you save not binge buying things.
- Shop every couple of days for fresh fruits and veggies or hit the farmer's market once a week! This will do several things. First, it will give you extra exercise. Second, you won't be filling your fridge with as much food, which means the potential for it to spoil is lessened. Third, if you shop farmers markets, you'll be supporting local farmers!
- Cut your meat. In the U.S., we're one of the few countries where meat is eaten at almost every meal. Really? You only need three ounces of lean protein per day. So why not cut back your meat eating to dinner only, and take one or two nights a week where you don't eat meat at all? Meat is expensive. At worst it will help both your pocketbook and your health, and perhaps even the planet.
- Brand names are more expensive. There's a reason I spend an average of $100 less when I don't shop at the big-name stores.

The smaller, independent stores don't always carry brand names and if they're into natural food, they don't carry a lot of junk food or crap you really don't need.

CLOTHING

- You probably don't need half of the clothing in your closet.
- If you do love clothes or you need a lot of different outfits for work, thrift stores are your friend. You can get gently used clothing at rock bottom prices if you look carefully.
- Learn how to mend so you can fix frayed hems or small rips. It will make your clothing go further.
- Get together with friends and have everyone bring their unwanted clothing items or clothing they're bored with. Then everyone can pick over each-others unwanted clothing and hopefully find some new pieces for their own wardrobe.
- Maintain your weight so you're not constantly having to buy new clothing or take clothes in or out.
- Limit the number of "DRY CLEAN ONLY" items in your closet. Dry cleaning is expensive.
- Unless you're an Olympic or competition athlete - you don't need more than one pair of exercise shoes. Buy one pair for what you do, or just get one pair of cross trainers.
- Keep everyday shoes practical and shop thrift stores for any excess. I have found that in a year's time I really only need one pair of cross trainers, one pair of casual walking shoes, one pair of dress shoes, a pair of boots, a pair of sandals, and one pair of heels for really special occasions. That's six pairs of shoes ladies. Six. I replace them every year or two depending on level of wear.
- Buy clothing items that multi-task and go with a lot of different things. That way you can wear it with different pieces in your wardrobe to get a different look. For the record - I own only one cocktail dress. Why? Because I go out someplace nice only a

few times a year. If you only go out maybe once or twice a year - you definitely don't need more than one or two.

ELECTRONICS

•	Only buy what you need and what you can afford. Does it really *have* to be a designer, brand-name computer? Or will a less expensive, more perks machine serve you just as well? Be honest! Sure, all of us may want the latest and greatest Apple i[insert device here], but there are less expensive alternatives that work just as well. Most phones nowadays serve as our streaming music devices and can be used to read eBooks and surf the web. There are also cheaper tablets out there that can do everything designer tablets do.
•	Use layaway plans instead of credit to purchase more expensive items. You'll save money on interest.

CREDIT CARDS

•	Credit card companies make more money on interest if you're in debt. That's where they want you.
•	Only keep ONE card. The one with the lowest interest rate is your best option. That means all those store cards need to be cut up. They often charge high interest rates.
•	Don't charge more than you can pay off the following month.
•	Pay it off every month.
•	Don't use credit if you can pay cash or put something on layaway.
•	Don't carry your credit card around with you or you'll be more tempted to use it. Keep it in a safe at home and only use it for emergencies or as necessary. On that note, don't save your credit card on the computer because it might make it easier for you to binge shop.

SAVINGS ACCOUNTS

- Get one.
- Treat it like a monthly bill and pay into it.
- Make sure you meet the minimum activity requirements. Some banks, if a savings account is inactive for a month, will start taking out "fees". Once this starts, your savings account can disappear quickly. Remember that banks are a business. They will try to get as much money away from you as possible. Use them, most certainly, but never trust them and watch them closely.
- Put as much as you can afford into savings. I suggest putting about as much as you spend on your cell or cable bill into savings every month. You really can't go wrong saving.
- Don't dip into it. Resist.
- You should stockpile enough money in your savings so that if you find yourself unemployed - you can live frugally for about six months. Some sources are now recommending sixteen months. That's not always realistic, but if you can do it - do it.

BANK ACCOUNTS

- I am not a fan of commercial banks because most of them will "fee" you to death. There's a fee for everything under the sun usually. Make sure you are aware of all fees and ALWAYS read the fine print.
- Try a local credit union first.
- Always keep a minimum balance in your checking account. I suggest $500-$1000. This way you won't accidentally overdraw and end up with bounced check fees etc.... Once you hit your minimum balance - train yourself to think you're broke.

BUYING A HOME

- Realtors will always try to get you into a more expensive home based on what a mortgage lender is willing to lend you. This is an issue and let me tell you why -- people lose their jobs. You may be able to afford a $2000 mortgage this month while you and your significant other are gainfully employed. But what happens a year from now when one of you loses their job? My rule of thumb - whichever of you makes the least - your wages should be able to cover a mortgage, heat/electricity, water and food. Everything else be damned if need be. If the lowest wage earner in your household can't pay those basic necessities, the mortgage is too expensive, and you need to shop for a less expensive home.
- Figure out what you can afford BEFORE you start shopping for a home, tell your Realtor your limit (not the bank's) and only look at homes within your limit. When my husband and I bought our house, I figured we could afford something around $220,000 based on my annual income. At the time I was the lowest wage earner. My Realtor kept trying to get us into $280K-$320K homes - what the mortgage lender approved us for. I kept pulling him back down to that $220K figure. We ended up buying a home under $220K. Sure enough, my husband lost his job a year later and was out of work for eight months. Because of our foresight, we were able to keep up on our mortgage and we didn't lose our home. Just because a bank approves you for more doesn't mean you have to go that high - and you probably shouldn't!
- Never, ever get a loan with a fluctuating interest rate. FIXED interest rate is the key phrase. Also stay away from second mortgages and arms. A home equity line of credit is not a bad thing, but if you're going to have one, keep it for home emergencies or upgrades and make sure you can pay it off in a timely manner! Most of them have a clause that says you must pay it off in full within ten years.

SHOPPING TIPS

- Watch for sales.

- Use coupons, but only for things you actually use! Don't just buy something because you have a coupon.
- Just because you have money to spend, doesn't mean you should.
- Only buy stuff in bulk if it's cheaper and it's something you use often.
- Go in with other family members or friends on buying in bulk.
- Use layaway when possible.
- Plan for upcoming expenses by saving for them (birthdays, holidays, etc...)

COSMETICS

- Cosmetics are expensive. Watch for sales or coupons for your favorite brands.
- Try to find cheaper brands for items you go through faster. (I know how hard this is, I have really sensitive skin.)
- The natural look is in! Using less makeup goes a lot further. So, try to use less when you can!
- There are cheaper shampoos and lotions that work just as well as the brand name stuff; though I still haven't found a substitute for my favorite shampoo. I keep trying.

HOLIDAYS

- If you have a large family, throw everyone's name in a hat and have everyone draw a name for the holidays. That way each of you only has to shop for one person instead of twenty.
- For birthdays, consider having everyone contribute a small amount to one big present for the person whose birthday it is.
- Make family gatherings potluck.
- Fancy centerpieces are optional. If you must, go outside, collect some pine cones and sticks, and glue them together (along with some googly eyes) to make little snowmen or whatever. Be creative. You don't need to buy silly little doodads that you only use once a year.
- Limit your decorations to one large plastic tote for each holiday. If you want something new - something from your current stash has to go. Chances are you'll reconsider your splurge purchase.

LEARN TO MAKE DO

- Used furniture stores have some great tables. So what if they don't match? Is the Pope coming for a visit? They're functional and function outweighs looks every time if you want to be debt free. Chances are no one is going to notice or care anyway. Hopefully your family and friends visit your home to see you -- not whether or not you have matching tables. If they must match - paint them.
- Use blankets, small appliances, and furniture until it absolutely must be replaced. Most Americans tend to replace things when they start to *look* ratty, or you want to replace them just because they're old. By keeping things a little longer, we can keep from having to buy new stuff longer. Garage sales are also a good place to shop for less expensive furniture.

- Yeah, so raking and bagging leaves sucks and having a new leaf sucker-vacuum might save you hours of work. But physical labor is good for you and it's a bit cheaper. The rule of thumb: if you can do it yourself without high tech equipment or hiring it out -- do it.
- Justify every purchase. If you take nothing else away from this chapter - consider that little statement. If you have to, make pro and con lists of major purchases. Do you really need the giant flat screen? Probably not. Sure, you want it - who doesn't? But it is not necessary for your survival, and being able to eat and pay your bills is far more important.
- Window shopping can be dangerous for those with little willpower. If you have impulse control issues (only you know if you do or not) - find a different hobby. Preferably one that doesn't cost a lot.
- You don't need Starbucks! Make your own coffee at home and add flavorings to it if you must. The five-dollar coffee is ridiculous. If you spend five bucks for a coffee more than once a month - you're spending money frivolously. Let's say you spend $5 20 days a month. That's $100 bucks. It adds up.
- Take your lunch to work instead of eating out. You can usually cut the cost of your lunch in half, and you can eat a lot healthier.
- Security systems, satellite radio, cable television, internet (unless you need it for work), cell phones (unless you don't have a land-line), and stuff like that -- all optional during a financial crisis. These are bills most of us have that can be cut right off the top if you're really in a bind. It amazes me how many people refuse to do it and would rather rack up the debt, have everything turned off, and then be sent to collection.
- A land-line (i.e. hardwired phone in your house) is cheaper than a cell phone. You know, people lived just fine without cell phones not more than 20-30 years ago. Unless you're a doctor or someone very important who needs to be accessible 24/7 (most of us are not, sorry) -- you really don't need a cell phone. Most cell bills are $70+ a month. That's a minimum of $840 a year you spend

just so your friends can call you no matter where you are. It really is a *want*, and it's expensive. Don't tell me, "Oh, but I have kids!" Yeah, my parents and your parents and our grandparents had kids, too. They didn't have cell phones back then and they seemed to be able to parent just fine without them.

TRANSPORTATION

- Walk, ride your bike, or take a bus or other public transportation whenever you can. Not only will you get more exercise, but you'll save on gas.
- Some people have no choice but to own and drive a car. Combine as many trips into one trip as possible to save on both gas and time. Not to mention you'll save wear and tear on your car, too.
- Carpool when possible.
- There is really no reason to own a huge pickup truck unless you actually haul a lot of stuff. I can't believe how many people I see who drive big pickups or gas guzzlers as commuter vehicles. If you're really serious about saving money, a fuel-efficient commuter car is key. Of course, if you have a huge family, then I totally understand the mini-van or SUV that seats 6-8 people. I just don't understand it when the only person I see in it day after day is the person driving and no one else.

CHILDREN

- Kids are really expensive. If you're a parent you already know this. If you're not -- keep that in mind when family planning or considering methods of birth control.
- Some parents buy their kids whatever they want. Teach your children early the value of a dollar by having them do chores for an allowance and then have them save for big purchases like the video game system they want. They'll learn valuable skills

that will last them a lifetime (for example, the skill of saving for what they want, which seems to be something we've lost).

- Shop thrift stores for school clothes when possible. While this may not always work, especially for items like shoes, it can help you stretch your clothing dollar. Especially since kids grow like weeds.

- Watch for sales and deals on school supplies. This seems like a no-brainer, but I've actually met parents who don't do this simple thing and then cry about how much school supplies cost them.

- Start saving for the following year's school supplies and fees in January.

- Don't always buy your kids what they want as a reward or just to get them to shut up. They'll start taking the value of a dollar for granted.

- Try putting together some sort of daycare swap with other parents you can trust in your neighborhood. You're not the only parent out there who finds the rising cost of daycare a financial nightmare. Some women work full time just so they can afford daycare. If you're working a job just to pay for daycare - why are you working at all? The idea of a daycare swap works something like this: Jane, Mary, and Sue all have two children each. Sue is a stay at home mom, Mary works from home, and Jane works 5 days a week. In the morning, Sue takes all the kids to school and watches the little ones who are too young to go to school. At three, she takes all the kids to Mary's (since Mary is done working for the day). On weekends and some evenings Jane watches all the kids to give Sue and Mary a break. And the parents may exchange money for snacks or gas or whatever the kids might need while they're watching each other's kids. Here's the deal - everyone has to watch the kids at some point. It can't be just one or two parents doing all the work while the other parents are merely reaping the benefits. If anyone backs out more than three times in a row, their kids are automatically expelled from the babysitting swap. Yeah - this isn't going to work for everyone, but for some people it might. It might also be cheaper to pay your retired mother, or a relative you trust who doesn't work, to watch the kids a few hours a day rather than to pay the local daycare.

COLLEGE

I actually read somewhere recently that most kids who go to college now will not be able to find jobs that pay enough money so that they can afford to pay off their student loans. This means we're simply driving more people to debt before they even get started in life. This same article said it's almost more advantageous (money-wise) for kids to seek out trade careers (electricians, plumbers, etc...) that provide on-the-job training instead of going to college. It's something to consider with more and more jobs going overseas where labor is cheap and plentiful.

- Texbooks: shop around for them if you can. College textbook prices are brutal. The more prestigious or specialized the school, the more expensive the books. Some books are proprietary, too, and can only be purchased in the college bookstore (usually because they're written by the professor teaching the class). My own nephew paid over $800 for one textbook. Figure this into your college financial planning.
- Computers: waiting until right before school starts to buy a computer is your best bet. Why? Some colleges require students use Macs and they have, again, proprietary software that is created to run on the latest, greatest machine (usually because they're also a distributor of said machines). You don't want to accidentally buy a system that won't run the software you need to run for your classes. So specifically find out what you need before you buy.
- If you have dreams of your kids going to college, start accounts for them early on. Savings accounts don't often accrue much in interest. If you want something that will give you more interest for your saving dollar, talk to your financial adviser about special investment accounts you can open up for your kid(s), so

whatever you put in will actually have the potential to grow. It's best to start such accounts when they're little.

- A lot of students complete their general study core at cheaper community colleges and then transfer their credits to a bigger university for the remaining requirements for their degree. Consider doing this. It makes a lot of financial sense.
- Try choosing schools in-state and close to home so you can live at home while attending school. This can really cut a college bill. Most schools with a "live on campus" requirement for freshman will waive that requirement for students who live close enough.
- Apply for a lot of scholarships. You never know where you might be able to get a few extra dollars to help you out.
- Work study programs can help decrease a tuition bill. Not to mention going to school full time can suck and it's nice to have a job to go to. Or at least I thought it was.

GENERAL FINANCE TIPS

- We are a capitalist society. This means greed runs rampant. Yes - everyone is out to get your money and take it from you in any way they can. It's not paranoid; it's just a fact of life.
- Never jump into any financial arrangement without reading the fine print.
- Pay your bills on time to avoid late fees or getting behind to where you can never catch up! Not to mention bad credit can keep you poor for life.
- Take care of your needs first. The bills always get paid before you get to go have fun. Sorry folks, this is what being an adult looks like.
- Treat everything like a scam until you understand it completely.
- There is no get-rich-quick scheme. Hard work, creative ingenuity, smart money management, and thinking before spending will get you further faster.

GETTING OUT OF FINANCIAL TROUBLE

- Consumer credit counseling services are usually non-profit and will work as a mediator between you and your creditors to get your debts paid off without all the excess interest. Once you have finished with the agreed upon payment plan, try to keep yourself out of hot water by following some of the tips in this chapter to control your spending.
- Define areas where you're in the most trouble. Is it credit card debt? If so, make a commitment to pay so much per month on the bill and follow the plan religiously. In the meantime, shred the card or lock it away.
- Medical debt is evil. The only way to overcome it is to make payment arrangements and stick to those payment arrangements.
- Try to pay everything that isn't a NEED by cash. If you don't have the cash, too bad.
- Make a budget plan and stick to it. This means you write down all your monthly bills (include your savings! and don't forget allowance for clothes and entertainment). Classify each bill as a need or a want. Then, write down how much money you make. Subtract your "Needs" bills from your income (savings is a NEED). Whatever is left over can be used for wants. If you have too many wants and not enough money for wants left over - cut them. For example, cable television is a want.
- It may be tempting to take out a loan to pay off your debt, but this won't work if you keep racking up debt on your credit cards.
- Wants come secondary to needs always. (Yes, I'm repeating this on purpose!)

INSURANCE
(for those who can afford it)

This mostly applies to Americans because I'm not sure people in other countries have this much issue with their insurance.

- You should probably have it. It's a **necessary** evil whether it be home, renters, car, medical or life.
- Shop around for insurance to get the best rate. Ask your friends who they use, if they've ever processed a claim and how well the insurance company processed the claim.
- When it comes to life insurance, learn the differences between whole life or term life. Term life policies are cheaper, but the coverage expires when you reach a certain age or after a certain amount of time has passed. Whole life policies, once they have a value, can be borrowed against if necessary and will be around until the day you die, but they're wicked expensive and you often have to go through a health screening to get them. Your best bet it to buy whole life while you're still young and relatively healthy.
- Health insurance is a need. It is expensive, yes, but if your family has a long history of various illnesses, it's better to be safe than sorry. Sometimes it's cheaper to pay $15,000 a year, $20 co-pays and a $5000 deductible than it is to pay for chemotherapy out of pocket. Just sayin'... On the flipside of that -- if you're really healthy, health insurance is just flushing money down the toilet. It's a crapshoot. You can get sick without health insurance, put yourself and/or your family into serious debt the rest of everyone's life, or you can have health insurance and never get sick. Some people argue that it might be a better bet to sink $15,000 a year into a health savings account for all the year's you're healthy (and can afford it) and then take really good care of yourself. But that's not necessarily a guarantee that it will be enough money to keep you going if you end up in the ICU for a few weeks. You just don't know. Health insurance is a mess here in the U.S., and until it's fixed, it can destroy you financially at any time.

THE FINAL WORD ABOUT MONEY MANAGEMENT

Now is about the time someone screams, "So you're telling me that in order to survive during lean times I have to live like a poor person?" Well, I suppose. Some of the wealthiest people in the world don't live extravagantly. I'm just suggesting we all start living within our means and making smarter financial choices to help us in the long run. I hope this chapter has helped you with some financial advice that will hopefully help you get out of debt, keep you from getting into debt in the first place, or give you a few tips on making your dollar go further.

Financial Budget Worksheet

EXPENSES (Next to each item, write down how much each item costs you every month.)

HOME
- Rent/Mortgage
- Renters/Homeowners Insurance
- Utilities
- Internet, Cable, Phones
- Other Housing Expense (Property Tax)

FOOD
- Groceries
- Eating Out
- Other

TRANSPORTATION
- Bus or Taxi
- Gas
- Parking and Toll Fees
- Car Maintenance
- Car Insurance
- Car Loan
- Other

HEALTH

- Medicines
- Health Insurance
- Vision Expense
- Dental
- Other

FAMILY AND FUN
- Child Care
- Child Support
- Clothing and Shoes
- Laundry
- Donations
- Entertainment
- Other

FINANCE
- Bank Fees
- Credit Card Fees
- Prepaid Cards and Phones
- Savings account (treat it like a monthly bill if possible)
- Other

OTHER
- School Expense
- Other Payments
- Other Expenses

TOTAL EXPENSES (add them up):

INCOME
- Wages after taxes and fees:
- Other Income:

TOTAL INCOME (add it up):

Now take your income and subtract your expenses. If your expenses exceed your income – find areas to cut and do this until your income exceeds or matches your expenses.

CHAPTER 11
FIVE DAEMONS FOR WEALTH AND SUCCESS

I didn't include this chapter earlier because I was hoping you'd read the first part of the book before really jumping into prosperity magick. The Daemons for prosperity and financial gain are numerous. After all, the Abrahamic religions found/find the acquisition of wealth both appalling and sinful (unless you're the church, of course). Hence the reasons there are so many Daemons, in Christian made pantheons and Judeo-Christian inspired grimoires, that rule over financial prosperity.

When you work with the Daemonic - you are consenting to being taught life lessons. That's just part of the unspoken bargain in working with ANY Daemonic force. This is how they've gotten such an "evil" reputation. So, it's not far-fetched to think they could be trying to make a point, or teach you a lesson (especially if you have any business dealings that aren't on the up-and-up - they will make you atone for that kind of stuff), with all the failure. Daemons love teaching lessons and forcing us to face our fears. It's part of their charm (or evil, depending on one's perspective).

Belial – Earth elemental, abundance, physical possessions. Monetary gain.
Color: Green or Brown
Direction: North or West
Element: Earth
Enn: *Lirach Tasa Vefa Wehlc Belial*
Sigil of Belial:

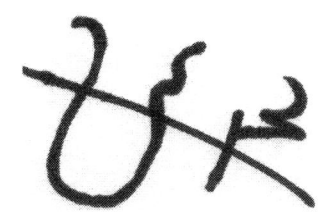

Belial is an obvious choice here considering he is the earth element. Earth is the element associated with physical possessions, finances, and abundance. In many of the old Christian generated hierarchies Belial was described as a Prince of inequity, that is bad behavior, and father of lies (Beliar). He has also been associated with arrogance. However, from a Demonolatry perspective, he is none of these things.

Belial is more active. He draws opportunities to you that will help bring abundance and security into your life. These are not the only things Belial is good at. The earth element also rules over stability, fertility, nurturing and things of that nature. But he only deals with physical pleasure, comfort, and security. Because earth is often viewed as a mother figure, some people view Belial as female. Obviously, we know Daemons do not have genders, but know that if you feel Belial in its "feminine" form, there's nothing wrong with that.

Belial is also one of the Ba'al deities. Some practitioners argue that his true name is Ba'al El. All of the Ba'al deities tend toward ruling over manifestations in the physical realm.

Belphegor - Mastery, gain, money, armor
Color: Green or Gold
Direction: North
Element: Earth
Enn: Lyan Ramec Catya Ganen Belphegore
Sigil of Belphegor:

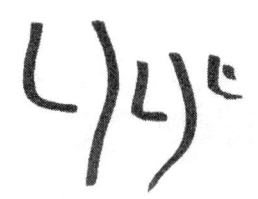

The problem with Belphegore is that he is a passive force when it comes to financial success. Belphegore brings to fruition works already put into motion. So, for example, if you're already looking hard for that dream job - he simply facilitates the opportunity by making sure your resume is seen by the right person. Or if you're a writer or musician and have books or music already done - Belphegore could assure you will get more royalties or an opportunity for recognition. If you have nothing going on and you seek Belphegore for quick cash, he might just kill off a favorite relative to give you "free" money. So be careful of this and try to be rather specific when working with him. Belphegore can also be invoked to make sure the job you have is stable and you're able to keep a roof over your head. Sadly, lasting wealth isn't passive or opportunistic which is how Belphegor works. That said - save Belphegore for opportunities and power boosts to things you already have going on.

Let's also take a moment to examine some of Belphegore's other attributes. Mastery: Belphegore's purpose is to help you become a master of your own financial life. This is why he is a passive force and will only bring success to people who are actively working toward mastering their own financial success. Gain and money are no-brainers. But some people may be confused by the word armor. Armor: in this sense Belphegore helps protect people from financial ruin. And often times this protection comes from mastery.

Despite his passive nature, Belphegore sometimes comes off as having aggressive energy. If you have a lot of fire in your elemental composition, or a lot of earth, you probably will not feel this way.

Mammon - Wealth and material gain.
Color: Gold
Direction: Northeast
Element Airy part of earth
Enn: Tasa Mammon on ca lirach
Sigil of Mammon:

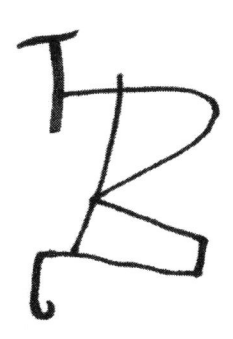

There is a reason Mammon is not strictly an earth element. Wealth and material gain require intelligence, and careful thought and planning. This is where Mammon shines. He can help the practitioner find wealth and material gain through careful planning and careers that are more cerebral. Scientists, doctors, investment bankers, accountants, lawyers, etc. can make great strides working with Mammon. If your plan to wealth requires a great deal of intelligence to pull off, Mammon is the Daemon you want to work with.

The one thing about Mammon though is, unlike Belial, the alchemical composition of his energy is not always pleasant for some magicians. As humans we often view this as a Daemon not liking us, or being foreboding or aggressive. Each magician's experience here will likely differ from his colleagues'. A lot of the energy we feel coming off of Daemons, we naturally translate it into an equivalent human emotion because that's how we can better comprehend what that energy feels like. Therefore, foreboding aggressive energy often comes off as hatred or dislike.

Sorath: Spirit of the sun whose number translates to The Black Sun. Fame, success, wealth.
Color: Gold
Direction: South
Element : Fire
Enn: Eva an ca Sorath Aken
Sigil of Sorath:

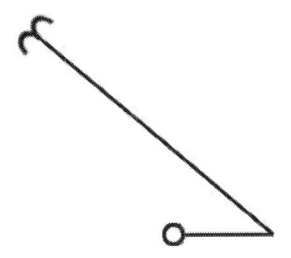

Sorath is one of those Daemons who can bring a great deal of fame to the practitioner. Please see the entire section about Sorath to learn more about the dangers and cautions of working with him. There's a reason I devoted an entire section to. Work with Sorath at your own risk and with extreme preparation and caution. I know it's tempting to want to jump right into the fire, just remember that fire burns.

Clauneck: Manifestation of goods, money, and finances.

Color: Silver
Direction: North or Northeast
Element: Airy part of Earth
Enn: Evna ana se nac Clauneck.
Sigil of Clauneck:

Money is not the only area in which Clauneck can be a useful Daemonic force to work with. Clauneck judges magicians by their own merit, and may weigh the magician's knowledge, with his passion, and how emotionally stable he or she is in matters of money and good judgement therein. It is from there that he can truly make manifest the magician's desire for goods, and money. This means that the magician should know himself rather well when working with Clauneck. This Daemon often teaches us something about who and what we surround ourselves with, and how that translates to the manifestation of our own success. He assesses our judgment and reveals it to us. This also suggests that he will not "work" for all magicians who invoke, summon, conjure, or evoke him. This Daemon picks and chooses who is worthy of his influence. While most Daemons do this to some degree, Clauneck's judgment is more refined.

Clauneck can also be invoked in matters of health (both physical and psychological), but the same rules apply. Clauneck will show the magician all of his shortcomings, explain the options, and leave him with the choice of how to proceed. It is then up to the magician to choose which path to take. If you're looking for a demon to tell you why you are not good with your money, or why you're not rich, Clauneck will lay it all out for you. Be careful because sometimes the truth hurts. You can lie to others, but you can't lie to yourself or the Daemonic Divine.

My suggestion is that one should always petition Clauneck first, to see if he is willing to work with you, before actually invoking him. Also, be sure you are ready for a dose of harsh reality, especially if you're deluding yourself about your goals regardless what area in life those goals may be focused on.

In closing, Clauneck is the Daemon who holds a mirror up to you and makes you take a long, hard look at yourself and your faults. This can be extremely helpful when it comes to prosperity magick.

I know the chapter is called Five Daemons for Wealth and Success, but then why is the seal of Seere on the cover? Because Seere is a Daemon of "finding" when it comes to wealth and prosperity, and this book is your map to finding prosperity. If you need to find something, Seere will reveal it.

Seere: Finding treasure and wealth.
Color: Gold
Direction: South
Element: Fire tempered with Earth
Enn: Jeden et Renich Seere tu tasa
Sigil of Seere

The way in which Seere brings the magician wealth and gain is to reveal something. To shed light on an area you've overlooked. To tap you on the shoulder and point you to a new opportunity. However, just as quickly, Seere can help you hide things from thieves, and reveal thieves as well. Many people find Seere to be an amiable Daemonic force willing to work with most people who approach her (or him depending on your association). She works under Amaymon (one of the great Daemons of desire, of the Asmodai) in the East. So, to work best with her, be sure that what you ask of her is what you desire most of all. Then let her show you the way.

One of the traditional methods of working with Seere is this: for those who have the gift of sight, you would sit in front of a scrying mirror, ball, or bowl, invoke her using her Enn, and then drink one eighth of a cup of Salvia Divinorum tincture. Seere will give you visions, revealing that which will best serve you. Now the problem with that formula is it may not be a good idea to jump to that much Salvia Divinorum in one shot. You need to start out small and take the smallest effective dose when working with those types of divination tinctures. After all, the point isn't to trip balls - it's to see what you're missing. Most clairvoyants need just enough of a substance to trip the darkness and go beyond the fade. Salvia and Wormwood tinctures work well with Seere. I've tried both. Wormwood is easier to get, but both can be just as effective. To learn more about tincturing herbs, see *Wortcunning for Daemonolatry*. That book also has plenty of incense and oleum recipes for monetary gain.

CHAPTER 12
SORATH

This chapter was included because so many magicians want to skip the rest and go straight to the big guns because they've heard that Sorath is where it's at.

Sorath is not a Daemon to jump into the fire with readily. One must give Sorath deep consideration before whipping out the candles and incense. The problem with Sorath, the intelligence of the sun, is that when you draw the sun's light to you unprepared - you're going to get burned. This is why a lot of people who work with Sorath either wither away, or find their most intimate secrets or embarrassments revealed. Sorath shines a spotlight on you and your work and will make you question your own validity, your actual skill or talent, and ultimately whether or not you can take the heat of fame. Not everyone fares well in the spotlight, and this is where people, especially creatives, need to be careful.

Sorath's light is so bright that he will attract critics, haters, trolls, and other vermin to you. Not to mention your schedule may become more hectic or even harrowing. If done right, bringing Sorath into a situation will make it so everyone wants a piece of you. Whether it be interviews, public appearances, or contract offers. You will truly find out quickly if you can hack it (or not). That is why you'll often find that smart magicians work with Sorath IN

TANDEM with other Daemonic forces to temper some of that heat and to cool the flames a bit. If you don't do this, it's very possible you'll end up a burnt-out husk cowering in a corner.

I know this because I've been there. I've worked with Sorath to catapult my fiction writing career to the next level, but I had done a great deal of research beforehand, including talking to other magicians about their own work with Sorath, that I knew going in that I would need to draw in other Daemonic influences as a "sunscreen" so to speak. I could go on about Sorath for pages and pages. He is one of those spirits one could write an entire book about.

I think you'll get the most out of Sorath from working with him. But again, don't rush too Sorath if this is your first ritual and you haven't given full consideration and preparation. I have included a few rituals here. First, I'll show you how to use Sorath and Paimon in tandem to boost productivity, and then I'll show you how to work with them to manifest the actual success and fame you seek.

Sorath Energy Draw
(for productivity)

I actually had a really rough time with figuring out how to draw Sorath for energy in the productivity department.

This particular ritual will help you draw in the energy from Sorath and use that energy for the productivity to do all the things that need to be done on your path to prosperity.

The key is you need to temper Sorath's influence because Sorath has a tendency to bring with him chaos. Chaos can be a productivity killer and the reason for that is because chaos distracts your focus. So many different things will happen at once that you will be unable to focus on the work itself, making it very difficult to be productive. So, if you're an artist, for example, you're going to want to temper Sorath with the Daemon Paimon. Because Sorath draws a lot of attention to one's work, his essence also draws the critics, trolls, and haters. In a business atmosphere, he may draw competitors, or those with sour grapes or jealousy. Paimon tempers this by destroying these obstacles and keeping gossip and the distraction of negativity to a minimum, helping the magician stay focused. This is why I have included the Paimon productivity booster below. You should do both of these rituals at the same time. You can bring in other Daemonic forces to temper the scalding light of Sorath, too. Myself and other magicians have just found that Paimon and Sorath seem to work very well together in this complementary way.

The goal here is to bring the energy of Sorath into your life and through you so that you can get as much done as possible. In a sense you could call this ritual The Drawing Down of Sorath. The ritual is done at mid-day (noon for our purpose) to draw on the energy of the sun. You can use more specific magickal timing based on the type of work you do, or the nature of what you wish to accomplish.

You Need:

- 1 Seal of Sorath
- 1 Magickal Oil of your preference

Bathe yourself at noon, then going to the temple with the sigil and your choice of magickal oil, whether it's dedicated to your profession or a Daemon of your choice. I prefer Abramelin oil. With this oil on your forefinger, draw the seal of Sorath on your chest. (As you can guess, you are nude at this point.)

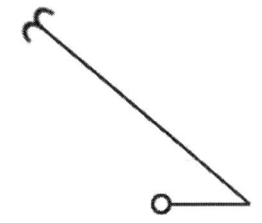

Sit down before the sigil and recite Sorath's Enn: *Eva an ca Sorath Aken*

Relax and draw yourself deep into meditation. Concentrate on the sigil. Feel free to recite the Enn as often as possible. Now imagine your energy extending out from the core of your being further and further from your body until it rises up into the atmosphere and encompasses the sun. Do this slowly until your energy and the sun's have merged. Now imagine drawing the energy of the sun back to you, pulling it back and back until you draw the essence of your energy back inside yourself. This process can take 20 to 30 minutes. After this is done, you will want to perform the Paimon productivity booster.

Paimon's Productivity Booster

Oftentimes people get sidetracked by other people, whether it be gossip, criticism, or just worrying too much about what others are doing. When we're so fixated on what other people are doing, we are minding their business, not our own. Naturally, the first step before performing this ritual is to realize that you need to stop worrying about everyone else, at least for now, because it only detracts from your own work. That's what the haters want. They want you to give them your undivided attention. They want your world to revolve around them. This is not healthy, and it keeps you from moving forward. This is why social media can have such a negative emotional impact on people. Don't be one of those people who, ten years from now, looks back at all the time you wasted minding everyone else's business when you should have been minding your own, and tending to your own prosperity.

Paimon can help here by stopping any gossip, and removing the distractions/obstacles (oftentimes other people). These are two things Paimon is very good at. Yes, Paimon has other talents, but for the scope of this book, these are the aspects of his nature that we're working with. The most important aspect being smashing obstacles, and in this case, the things holding you back from productivity.

You need:

- The seal of Paimon
- a piece of paper
- a piece of tape (or two)
- a pen
- offering bowl
- one candle (as a fire source)

On the piece of paper write down what you need to get done without distraction. Next, draw the seal of Paimon. Finally, make a list of the people or situations distracting you. Invoke Paimon over the piece of paper using his Enn: *Linan tasa jedan Paimon.*

Now, take a piece of tape (or two if you need it) and put it right over those distractions. Effectively, and symbolically diminishing the influence of these distractions. Finally, hold the piece of paper between your hands and delve deeply into meditation. I'm not going to describe how to go into the meditation here because each person goes into meditation in their own way. Once in the meditative state, I want you to imagine mountains standing before you. These mountains stand between you and all of your goals. With your mind, I want you to move these mountains, or smash them, and imagine the path before you clearing, so that you can see your end goal. Do this meditation until the mountains and obstacles have been removed, then walk toward your goals. You should spend no less than fifteen minutes performing this meditation, with the firm intent of being productive and working toward your goals.

After you've done this working, get up and go do whatever task or tasks you need to finish for the day.

Of course, don't expect the magic itself to keep you off of Facebook or Twitter, or whatever social media platform you may hang out on. Either turn off your Internet connection, or use a site blocking tool to block your access to those gateways, thus decreasing the likelihood that you will be distracted. Always follow magick up with real-world, tangible measures to help you. That's what I call *follow-through*.

The following ritual draws in a foundational "grounding" sigil of Sorath, along with the Daemon Paimon, to temper the fire. For more about my Sorath work, watch for my coming grimoire that details the making of the magickal model of Sorath, and how various influences can temper these flames. If you do it right - Sorath will catapult your work (whatever that work may be) into the spotlight.

SORATH & PAIMON WORKING FOR SUCCESS AND FAME

Sorath works in conjunction with the Sun and Saturn. Only those who have completed sufficient Saturn work can withstand the full manifestation of the Black Sun. Saturn, as a taskmaster who teaches hard lessons, teaches resilience, strength, and perseverance. A magician without these qualities will either have short-lived fame or they will be destroyed. So again, be warned. Some have claimed that invoking other planetary intelligences, like those of Jupiter, Neptune, or Venus will help to protect you while doing Sorath work. This is entirely up to you.

First you will make the seal.

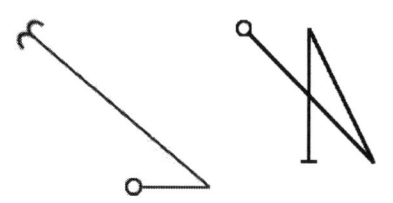

On a Thursday at 3PM or 10PM, create the seal. Either draw these sigils on opposite sides of a piece of paper (the foundational seal on one side, the active seal on the other) or make it of a more permanent material, small enough to be carried with you. Ideally you would want this to be more permanent, so you can draw, carve or burn the sigils on opposite sides of a small piece of circular wood, or carve them into a disk gold colored clay (one on one side, one on the other). You may also make the seal out of gold if you have skills in metallurgy. When you are finished making it - hold it on high, imagining the energy of the sun encompassing it and invoke Sorath: *Eva an ca Sorath Aken*

After it is initially made, immediately put it beneath your mattress and leave it there until morning.

The following morning, remove it from beneath the mattress and say over it, *"I summon you Sorath! Come forth and grant me the fame I desire! I wish to be famous for [state specific thing you'd like to be famous for here]! Grant me this and bring this to me!"*

If you aren't opposed to blood magick, feeding the sigil a drop of blood is fine. Each night, meditate over your seal for a minimum of an hour, imagining Sorath's light, the light of the black sun, filling the sigil. The sigil should feel energized and warm to the touch when you're finished. Afterward, place it beneath the mattress again. Repeat this process for a full seven days!

The whole point of this initial exercise is to fully attune the sigil to your intent and to make sure it's fully charged with the energy of Sorath by the time you perform the ritual.

On the following Thursday, you will perform the ritual at 3PM or 10PM. Bring the seal into the temple with you.

From the South, summon Sorath: *Eva an ca Sorath Aken*

From the North, summon Paimon: *Linan tasa jedan Paimon.*

Then say: *"Lord Paimon, lend your assistance to help temper the flames of Sorath as I seek my fame and success. Lead me away from conflict, and deliver me from gossip and tyranny."* Bow your head to him in respectful acknowledgment and thank him for his help.

Move back to the South - *"Come forth Sorath and draw your light to me! I stand in your fire, though I do not burn. Instead - I am reborn in your image, glorious and charismatic, full of energy and vitality! I draw you to me, great Sorath that you may crown me with the flames of my desire! So be it!"*

Hold the sigil on high, allowing Sorath to emblazon it with the fire energy of his nature, then draw it to your chest, thanking Sorath for the gift he's given you.

Stay in the temple as long as it feels right, then use this seal by carrying it with you, or bringing it to any magick or meditation you'll be doing as part of this Great Work.

This ritual can be redone once a month, and the seal recharged, until you reach your goals.

CHAPTER 13
WHY SELLING YOUR SOUL IS STUPID

As the title of this chapter suggests, here is the part where I talk about pacts because wealth and prosperity magick is where most folks have a tendency to want to throw a Daemonic pact at the problem. There are a lot of reasons pacts can be stupid on the road to financial gain. I talked a lot about this in my book *Daemonolater's Guide to Daemonic Pacts*. If you haven't read that book you probably ought to. A pact with a demon can help with small financial windfalls. But it is never a substitute for hard work, or sustainable and lasting wealth. You could make a pact for a financial windfall, or success in business, but be sure you're willing to follow through with your end of the bargain.

As I've said many times before, a pact is basically a deal you make with yourself. The Daemons are only there as "hired on" support staff. They help you hold yourself accountable to you. If you have no intention of following through, expect a Daemonic slap down, because that's essentially what you're "paying" them for.

The following is a general pact outline. I don't recommend you give up your soul or your first born, both of which are ridiculous offerings, but instead something you can actually agree to. For example, daily offerings, your undivided attention to their teachings, or a promise to work on yourself in some way. Daemons will often accept these things in place of souls or blood. By that I don't mean to say you can't use blood offerings. Pacts are often sealed with the magician's blood in the signature. And that's okay. Some Daemons will accept offered drops of blood in exchange for things, too. For example, I've offered to write books, or articles, on behalf of certain Daemons over the years in order to gain their help for something. Perhaps you will offer to compose music for them. Or make them a meal once a week for a month. Or perhaps you'll offer an hour of meditation with them each month. Talk to the Daemons and ask what they want in return to help you out.

If they mention harming yourself or someone else - that's likely not a Daemon you're communicating with. As always, use discernment. Actual Daemons (Divine Intelligence) will never ask you to harm yourself or another living thing. What they often get out of their working relationships with human magicians is attention, someone to impart their wisdom on, or the opportunity to help you grow. Believe it or not, the role of divine intelligence (Daemons) in the natural order of things is to elevate the beings who seek them out whether by teaching them, imparting wisdom, or helping the individual grow. While that may not seem like a huge payoff to us, the energy exchanged in that IS enough of a payoff for *them*. That's hard for some magicians to accept, especially since the human imagination loves fantastical stories about soul collecting Daemons, or dramatic war stories that plot good against evil.

That said, here is a sample pact for prosperity.

Daemons suggested: Belphegor, Ba'al, Belial

Suggested Pact Text:

I, _____ [your name], in deepest respect, do hereby offer [Daemonic Name] [what you intend to give the Daemon] in exchange for prosperity. [Enter other specifics here.]

I affirm a pact with You, [Daemon], is my most heartfelt desire. By signing and dating this pact below I do dedicate myself to the pursuit of prosperity. [add specifics here]. Below I affix my seal:

_____ [date]
_____ [signature with blood]

[Daemon's Seal]

Considerations: Consider altering this pact to be more specific about the prosperity you seek. Prosperity comes in all shapes and sizes. Prosperous ideas, prosperous health, prosperous knowledge, prosperous relationships. Also remember that the Daemon needs something to work with here. Especially if we're talking about monetary prosperity. In that case you better be good at your job, have a strong talent or skill, or a very rich relative (who likes you) close to death for a prosperity pact of that nature to manifest to its full potential. If you have none of these things and you want financial prosperity, you might pick a skill and try to develop it instead. Or work with Clauneck and have him help you figure out what the problem is.

CHAPTER 14
REASONS MONEY/SUCCESS MAGICK OFTEN FAILS

There are two main reasons magick for prosperity fails.

1. You didn't want it bad enough to make it a priority and therefore failed to change your habits or your feelings and did not follow through.
2. You have deep emotional ties to the sentence, "I can't because [insert excuse here]."

If you find yourself in a position where absolutely NONE of the magick outlined in this book works for you, you have one of two options. You can cuss me out and can give up and go back to searching for a magick key to cure all your ills, or you can work through those things holding you back, explore each one, and move forward. That likely means working through this book again. I want you to feel empowered and confident. I want every last one of you reading this to succeed in your goals and to live a life of prosperity and good fortune. You deserve that.

Which means you deserve to give yourself another chance, or as many chances as it takes. The only thing I ask is that you don't give up on the goal. If you are willing to do everything I ask of you in this book, and you're willing to work it — you WILL see some type of prosperous improvement. Many of you will be able to find success if you're faithful and have a strong work ethic.

I recently had a woman with a disability contact me in an email the size of a novelette, to tell me she could not do any type of magick for prosperity because she was limited in what she could do because of her retinal detachment. She couldn't buy ritual implements due to her fixed income. She couldn't do a ritual because she was legally blind. I explained to her that she could do the rituals in the astral temple - no physical ritual implements required. To which she replied that she still had no means to change her situation. All of this in pages and pages of prolific, beautiful prose. Being a writer myself, my natural thought was, *you're so blind you don't even see what a brilliant writer you are, and you could do astral work to excel and succeed in some type of writing vocation.*

I told her this, but alas, no. She completely ignored my compliments and suggestion. In that moment I felt sorry for her because at some point she'd convinced herself (or others had helped her convince herself) she was a victim and had no skills, no talent, and nothing to offer the world, and certainly no means to change her financial situation even though she clearly did.

I hope this story has made you look at your own situation with more clarity, especially if you've convinced yourself that you're a victim with no way out. You have something to offer the world that will bring you great prosperity (financial or other, depending on your definition). What is it? Figure out that riddle and this book becomes your key to turn past failures into future success.

Chapter 15
Common Self-Work Requirements for Successful Prosperity Work

One of the biggest problems with wealth magick is that people don't understand the underlying psychological work that needs to be done to change how we view wealth. So, for example, if you have always identified as a poor person and you have cultivated bad habits such as spending your money as quickly as you get it, you need to go through and remove those thought patterns and exchange them with more productive habits that serve your wealth. This can be a long and tedious process that can take years. A lot of times when we think about wealth, we think about having opulent things, meaning we measure wealth by the things that we have. Or we covet expensive things for social status.

We don't stop to think that maybe things aren't important. By that I mean maybe it's not so important to have diamond rings or expensive jewelry, or even large expensive watches inlaid with gold. When we remove how we think about luxury items, we can really end up saving a lot of money in the long run by only spending money on things that are actually important.

My husband and I, instead of spending thousands on a grand wedding and wedding rings, took that money and made a down payment on a house. In retrospect, it was a smart decision because real estate was a far better investment, and a better allocation of our resources. We understood what we valued and ended up making a choice that put us in a better financial position.

I want you to sit down and make a list of everything you value. Why do you want wealth? Do you just want fancy cars? Women to notice you? Are leather shoes and expensive suits things that will make you happy?

Chances are - no. Culturally we've been conditioned as consumers. We've been told that having expensive things is important if you want respect or power. So now we have to break down those conditioned responses and societal constructs, and realize that they're likely the very things keeping us poor.

When we start worrying about more important things, we can eliminate a lot of excess spending. I'm not saying you need to live like a pauper (unless you're trying to rein in your financial situation). Instead, I am suggesting that our priorities are skewed. Make a list of what you value, then go through and write down why you value each thing. What is your reason for valuing a $2,000 watch? Be honest here because no one will see this list except you. You can shred it or burn it when you're done.

Now go through your list of reasons and ask yourself: Is this a good reason? Or is it ridiculous? Who will be impressed? What would you gain from that impression? Does spending the money on the watch instead of something more important like a down-payment on a reliable vehicle, for example, further your financial security? Or does it just make you feel good or important?

So, understanding what we value and why we value it is the first step to changing how we think about money.

Next, we have to look at how we view money as a whole. Do we hate it? Do we avoid it? Do we even understand it? Do you understand how investing, interest, and the rest of it even works? How you feel about money can either hinder your magick or enhance it. Because, you see, culturally we tend to put a lot of value on the money itself and not what it affords us. This is why so many wealthy people won't just sit back and relax and enjoy what their money affords them, but instead keep working on getting richer and richer as if whoever dies with the most wins. It's like a disease.

You can't take it with you. Remember that. A friend of mine once told me, *"I thought money was something you aspired to have so you could retire and spend your twilight years relaxing, traveling, and spending time with those you love doing things you enjoy. Instead, I see wealthy people who never retire because they want more money! I don't understand."*

Another friend marveled at the ridiculousness of money itself. He said, *"Think about it. It's just a piece of paper. The reality is that it has no value whatsoever. We all just imagine it has value and use it to buy and sell so no one rapes and pillages. Hell, most of our money exists in our heads because we never see it. It's either in the cloud somewhere or on paper. It doesn't really exist at all."* Now if you were smoking weed when you read that — Mind. Blown.

But see — all of these crazy thoughts dictate how we view, work for, and spend our money. And this ultimately dictates how we perceive wealth, which affects our magickal work with a monetary end goal. Always remember that.

CHAPTER 16
MORE SPELLS AND RITUALS FOR PROSPERITY

A couple of these are repeated from some of my other books, but they warranted repeating here just to keep everything in one place for reference.

Belphegor for Opportunities

You Need:
- One Piece of Paper
- Pen
- 7 Diabetic Lancet Devices (one for each day)
- Fireproof Bowl

On a piece of paper draw the sigil of Belphegor and sign your name. Then, for the next week, once a night, take the piece of paper to a quiet place and say,

"Belphegor, I seek opportunity that I may [enter purpose here]. I invoke you! Lyan Ramec Catya Ganen Belphegor!"

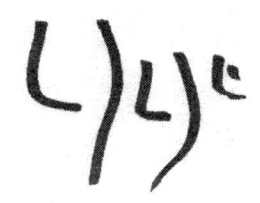

Then, using a diabetic lancet, prick your finger and put a drop of blood on the sigil. This is your blood offering to the Daemon. At the end of the week, burn the paper in a fireproof bowl and spread the ashes outside. You will have your new opportunities from 24 hours to 30 days after this operation. I've learned that Belphegor tends to work immediately for me. Within 24 hours. Others have said it can take a few days to start seeing opportunities roll in.

Ba'al and/or Belial Drawing Wealth Opportunities

Draw one of the two sigils below (Ba'al left and Belial right)

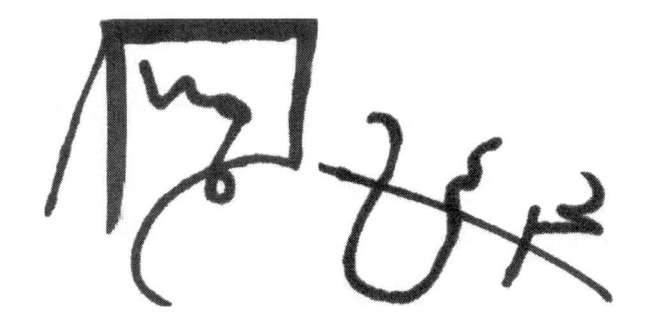

Now, give the seal(s) your desires. Write them down. Such as: I seek wealth through my sales job. I must become top salesman and rise up the ladder to become a VP of sales and draw a six-figure salary. I am willing to work for this wealth I will have. Show me the path!

Remember that being specific is important. The more specific you are and the better your outlined plan – the more likely you'll be successful.

Now imagine yourself as a wealthy person, and project that into the sigil(s). Carry the sigil(s) with you and look at them periodically. If you wish, you can make the sigils more permanent with clay, wood, or metal. You may also initially consecrate the seal with your blood to solidify your intent. But this is optional. I am told it works either way. I only work blood magick (using only my own blood, drop by drop) with these types of Daemonic force, but that's a personal choice.

Acquire A Job

This is a ritual I've performed for family and friends when they're experiencing a bout of unemployment. Please note it will only work IF you are actively seeking employment by filling out applications and sending out resumes. It always gives good results by producing interviews within a week of the ritual's performance. While I make no guarantees, I do dare the job seeker to try this ritual and see if you get the same results. When a dear friend was unemployed seven months, I did this ritual and he got three interviews the next day, one resulting in a job.

Invoke Belphegor thrice around the altar table (triangle ritual construct – gives proper energy). Take 4 pieces of parchment. In black, draw triangles on three and a circle on the fourth. Arrange them as such – one triangle at the top, the circle below it, and a triangle on the right and left of the circle. All the while – envision yourself or your unemployed family member or friend having a job. Now, draw the sigil of Belphegor in each of the triangles in green ink. Take three green candles (in candle holders) anointed with Belphegor oleum and place them on top of the parchments, inside the triangles. In the circle, draw the sigil of Belphegor, the name of the person to be employed (along with a drop of blood after their name), and the word EMPLOYMENT. Put a green stone or piece of glass in the circle. Place also in the circle a brown candle anointed with Belphegor oleum, but also engraved with the name of the person to be employed. Burn an incense of cloves and mint (or Belphegor incense or something comparable). Let the candles burn down. Have the unemployed person carry the stone/glass with them. Repeat this ritual every three days until employment is achieved, though usually the ritual only needs to be done once.

Financial Help

Financial windfalls are something everyone needs every now and again. To gain financial help first (outdoors) create a circle of stones about one foot wide. In the circle of stones carve the sigil of Belphegor or Ba'al Peor into the ground. Start the ritual by invoking Belphegor by employing his Enn: *Lyan Ramec Catya Ganen Belphegor,* then spilling a few drops of your blood in the center of the circle.

Next, place one drop of blood on a dollar bill. Put this above the main door of your house. Next, on a piece of parchment, draw the sigil of Belphegor. Around it, write specifically that you need a financial windfall and how you would like it to happen if you know. Burn this in the offering bowl while reciting Belphegor's Enn. Take the ashes of the burnt offering to your stone circle and leave them there.

Repeat this ritual for nine days straight. This will produce a financial windfall in a month's time.

Please note that if you are unspecific about what kind of windfall you'd like, that the windfall could happen in unsuspected ways. Such as a beloved relative dying. Or you may have an opportunity to sell something you love dearly at top dollar. So, consider this when allowing the Daemonic Divine choose the method of your financial help for you.

Nine Day "Get Money"

If you've been working traditional Daemonolatry for some time, you understand that there is an element of traditional witchcraft to some of the workings. This one may seem like a simple candle spell (with Daemons), but don't let its simplicity fool you. It's actually a powerful little spell. You can perform it at any time, day or night, but if you repeat it, try to do it at the same time each day. I recommend starting on a Thursday. Thursdays are good for monetary gain as they're ruled by the planet Jupiter, which can bring good fortune in the monetary department.

You need:

- 1 Green Candle
- 1 White Candle
- 1 Oil of Belphegor or Belial (Depending which Daemon you feel most drawn to, for recipes see *Wortcunning for Daemonolatry*. If you have neither, use cinnamon oil, or basil oil, both of which can easily be made by steeping these culinary herbs in some olive oil for a week or two.)

The green candle represents money or wealth. If you associate a different color with money, by all means, use that color instead. You are represented by the white candle.

The first step is to carve your name into the white candle. Then carve the name of Belphegor or Belial (choose the Daemon you feel most drawn to) into the green candle.

The second step is to anoint both candles with the oil (oleum) of the Daemon you're working with. Start at the center and work your way toward you when anointing.

While you're performing these first two steps, visualize the money you wish to receive. Be specific if you can be. This will infuse your intent into the candles.

Next, chant or vibrate the Enn of the Daemon you're working with over each candle three times. This should draw the Daemonic energy into the candles.

While I recommend you do "spell like" work within a prepared ritual space if you are a beginner, if you're more experienced and already know how these Daemons' energies affect you, you can skip it.

Next, place the candles upon the altar about one foot apart. Light them, then recite the Enn of the Daemon you're working with (see section on Daemons). Additionally, you can place the sigil of the Daemon you're working with between the candles.

Now you say over the candles:

"Money, wealth come to me,
In abundance come to me,
I draw upon the power of [Daemon Name]
To bring me prosperity.
So be it."

I know it's not a poem, but you're welcome to switch this up and add your own flair.

After you are finished, extinguish the candles and leave it on your altar. You will do this for nine nights, each time moving the candles closer together. By the ninth night they will be standing side by side. At this point you will let both candles burn until they burn to nothing. Be sure to focus on money every time you do this and don't get lazy and skip that part. You're focusing on your intent, and that's one of the most important parts here.

Yes, there is a nine Daemonic Divinities component here, which you can activate by acknowledging one of the nine Daemonic Divinities each night if you so choose. So, if you want to add a spiritual bend to this, perhaps say a small prayer of thanks to one of the nine Daemonic Divinities each night after you extinguish the candle. Will it help the magick? Probably. Is it necessary? Depends on your personal beliefs or leanings. I've known people who have done 7-9 day money candle spells that didn't involve spirits at all and it worked. Though I personally believe I get faster and better results drawing the Daemonic into this simple candle spell.

Money Multiplyer

This is a simple spell to help you draw more money to you. It's great for quick windfalls of cash. Take a fresh ten or twenty from your wallet. You can use smaller or larger bills, but most of us have a ten or twenty handy, and the idea behind this spell is that the bigger the bill you use, the more money you'll get. I suppose it works on the psychology that we think bigger with a bigger bill, thus drawing more money to us. You can also use more than one bill if you choose.

On a full moon - take a fresh #10 envelope and draw the sigil of a monetary Daemon (your choice, choose the one you're most comfortable with) on the outside of it. For those of you who practice blood magick, add a drop of your blood to the sigil.

Place the bill(s) into the envelope and seal it. Fold it in half towards you and say:

"[Daemon's Enn] [Daemon's Name] Hear me! I wish to multiply this money, quickly. I seek your influence. As it is done, so be it. Thank you."

You can change how you word this, but the gist is that you are asking the Daemon you're working with to help multiply the money through the influence of their energy. Remember to always thank the Daemon.

Repeat this once a day for up to two weeks using the same envelope, and as you do it, imagine more and more bills in the envelope. You may even feel it getting heavier. Keep this envelope beneath your mattress or in a drawer when you are not working the spell.

You should receive the money in that time. Once the money has manifested, you can open the envelope and put the money back into your wallet. Better yet - put it in your savings account.

To Make a Magickal Coin Talisman

Three days before a full moon, take a quarter from your pocket and wash and dry it. Let it sit in salt for three days to clear any negative energy on or around it.

On the full moon, take a bowl filled with rain water or melted snow (use purified water in a pinch) outside into the moonlight and drop the quarter into the bowl. Let the moonlight pour over it and imagine the lunar essence being soaked up by the quarter and imagine the quarter bringing money to you. You don't have to say any fancy words unless you need something to anchor your intent. If this is the case, try something like:

"By the Daemonic Divine, by Thoth and Seshat, draw wealth to me through this coin."

When you are finished with the visualization, pour the water onto the ground and let the earth soak it up, then dry off the quarter and keep it in your pocket or purse. Make sure you keep it separate from other change, so you don't lose track of it. Business owners may keep this quarter in their cash box in a small change envelope to decrease the chance of spending it.

The idea behind this as that you'll never be poor as long as you keep the quarter, and your coffers will always be full.

A Cord of Nine Money Spell

As we all know, prayer cords can be made for a variety of things. They can be devotional, but they can also be spells in and of themselves. For this one you will need either a dyed piece of leather (either green, gold, or brown) or a thicker silken cord in green, gold, or brown. It needs to be about fifteen inches long at least. The length will decrease significantly as you tie the knots.

Work with a Daemon or multiple Daemons of your choice. This cord will not only be serving your wealth, but will be harnessing their energy to help you.

Take up the leather or cord and starting at one end, you will tie a total of nine knots, and at each knot you will make a request.

With this first knot [Daemonic Name] brings opportunity.
With this second knot [Daemonic Name] brings work.
With this third knot [Daemonic Name] brings money.
With this fourth knot [Daemonic Name] brings more opportunity.
With this fifth knot [Daemonic Name] brings more work.
With this sixth knot [Daemonic Name] brings more money.
With this seventh knot [Daemonic Name] brings success.
With this eighth knot [Daemonic Name] brings permanence.
With this ninth knot [Daemonic Name] brings me wealth.
So be it.

Thank the Daemon(s) you've worked with. Keep this cord on your altar, or someplace where you can view it to remind you that success is yours.

Simple Candle Spell

If you haven't noticed, a lot of traditional Daemonolatry work is steeped in traditional witchcraft spellwork. This is no accident. The reason these spells have endured is because they work. Adding Daemonic force to the magick simply amps up the power of them.

Candle magick is some of the simplest forms of magick out there and it's relatively cheap and quite accessible for most people.

You Need:

- 1 Green Candle (or gold)
- 9 coins (doesn't matter what)
- A piece of green cloth (or gold)
- Cinnamon from the kitchen cupboard.
- Either a money drawing oil, or some olive oil
- A small athame or carving tool.

Alternatively, you can use brown or gold if you don't like the green = money association.

The entire time you do this ritual, envision your want (or need) for a financial windfall. Carve your name on one side of the candle. On the other side, carve the name BELIAL. Now anoint the candle with the olive oil, drawing the oil toward you (to signify money coming to you).

Light the candle and place the nine coins around the candle. Imagine all that energy from the candle drawing the money to you into the coins. Envision that you already have the money you're seeking. Let the candle burn down a bit.

Next, take the green (or gold) cloth and lay it out flat. Pick up the coins and place them in the cloth, then sprinkle the cinnamon on it. Imagine the power of Belial filling the cloth with money drawing energy.

If you have any money chants or invocations you want to use here - go for it. It's not necessary, but some people find it helps them focus.

Now fold up the edges of the cloth to create a small pouch for the coins and tie the ends so none of the coins escape. Let the candle burn down to nothing, then carry the pouch with you either in your pocket or your purse.

Note - use smaller charm candles so you don't have to wait hours and hours for the candle to burn down. You can also use a tealight. You'd simply carve your name and that of Belial around the wick, then anoint, and burn. It's still just as effective.

Spells like this aren't often meant for lasting wealth. They're simply meant to bring you windfalls of cash.

Some Folk Magick

Affix a dollar bill over the front door of your house (or business). As long as it's there, you will never be poor.

For Business: Keep the first dollar you earn and keep that above the shop door to draw business and to keep your business prosperous.

Bibliography and Suggested Reading

By S. Connolly:
- The Complete Book of Demonolatry
- Daemonolater's Guide to Daemonic Magick
- Daemonolater's Guide to Sex, Money, and Power
- Daemonolater's Guide to Daemonic Pacts
- Wortcunning for Daemonolatry
- Drawing Down Belial